The Confident School Leader

This exciting resource will help you build confidence in yourself as an educational leader. Written by an award-winning leader, this book encourages readers to use research-based strategies to lead in meaningful, authentic ways that make the greatest impact on students and staff members each day. Full of real-life stories and key takeaways, readers will walk away from this book with a better plan for reinvigorating their leadership skills and awaken the confidence within.

Whether you are a future administrator, a new principal, or a veteran administrator, the seven key leadership themes in this book will guide you in influencing and implementing change to effectively lead your school.

Dr. Kara Knight, Ed.D., is an award-winning educator and current Principal of Boone Trail Elementary School, MO.

Other Eye on Education Books Available from Routledge
(www.routledge.com/eyeoneducation)

Creating, Grading, and Using Virtual Assessments: Strategies for Success in the K-12 Classroom
Kate Wolfe Maxlow, Karen L. Sanzo, and James Maxlow

Leadership for Deeper Learning: Facilitating School Innovation and Transformation
Jayson Richardson, Justin Bathon, and Scott McLeod

A Practical Guide to Leading Green Schools: Partnering with Nature to Create Vibrant, Flourishing, Sustainable Schools
Cynthia L. Uline and Lisa A. W. Kensler

Rural America's Pathways to College and Career: Steps for Student Success and School Improvement
Rick Dalton

Bringing Innovative Practices to Your School: Lessons from International Schools
Jayson W. Richardson

A Guide to Impactful Teacher Evaluations: Let's Finally Get It Right!
Joseph O. Rodgers

A Guide to Early College and Dual Enrollment Programs: Designing and Implementing Programs for Student Achievement
Russ Olwell

The Strategy Playbook for Educational Leaders: Principles and Processes
Isobel Stevenson and Jennie Weiner

Unpacking Your Learning Targets: Aligning Student Learning to Standards
Sean McWherter

Strategic Talent Leadership for Educators: A Practical Toolkit
Amy A. Holcombe

Becoming a Transformative Leader: A Guide to Creating Equitable Schools
Carolyn M. Shields

Working with Students that Have Anxiety: Creative Connections and Practical Strategies
Beverley H. Johns, Donalyn Heise, Adrienne D. Hunter

Implicit Bias in Schools: A Practitioner's Guide
Gina Laura Gullo, Kelly Capatosto, and Cheryl Staats

The Confident School Leader

7 Keys to Influence and Implement Change

Kara Knight

First published 2022
by Routledge
605 Third Avenue, New York, NY 10158

and by Routledge
2 Park Square, Milton Park, Abingdon, Oxon, OX14 4RN

Routledge is an imprint of the Taylor & Francis Group, an informa business

© 2022 Taylor & Francis

The right of Kara Knight to be identified as author of this work has been asserted in accordance with sections 77 and 78 of the Copyright, Designs and Patents Act 1988.

All rights reserved. No part of this book may be reprinted or reproduced or utilised in any form or by any electronic, mechanical, or other means, now known or hereafter invented, including photocopying and recording, or in any information storage or retrieval system, without permission in writing from the publishers.

Trademark notice: Product or corporate names may be trademarks or registered trademarks, and are used only for identification and explanation without intent to infringe.

Library of Congress Cataloging-in-Publication Data
A catalog record for this title has been requested

ISBN: 978-0-367-64092-7 (hbk)
ISBN: 978-0-367-64463-5 (pbk)
ISBN: 978-1-003-12462-7 (ebk)

DOI: 10.4324/9781003124627

Typeset in Warnock Pro
by codeMantra

To all who have doubted themselves or failed greatly. May you find the confidence to rise again to be the leader you are called to be.

Contents

Meet the Author — xi
Acknowledgments — xiii
Introduction — 1

▶ Key 1

Lead with Authenticity — 5
Let Authenticity Lead the Way — 6
Leaders Lead Themselves First — 9
Creating a Personal Vision — 10
Unexpected Times Can Deliver Excellence — 11
Your Vision — 12
Questions for Reflection — 14
Dashes of Honesty — 15
Building on Shifting Rock — 17
True Authenticity — 20
Never Perfect, Always Authentic — 21
Are You Growing to the Leader You Wish to Be? — 23
3 Key Takeaways — 24

▶ Key 2

Understand Your Influence — 27
The Keys Are Yours — 28
Failing with Commitment — 30
Failure-Tolerant Leadership — 31
Intention Is Everything — 32
Your Influence Effect — 32
Looking into the Business World — 33
Slow Down, When You Can — 35
Your Interest, Your Influence — 37
Mind, Heart, & Team — 40
Leader Lightbulb Moment — 41
Growing Confidence — 43
3 Key Takeaways — 44

▶ Key 3

Trust Your Gut	47
People Pleasing	49
You May Be a People Pleaser If You	50
An Overflowing Profession	50
What Is Intuitive Cognition, You Say?	51
Intuitive Decision-Making	52
Check Yourself Before You Wreck Yourself	56
How Do I Gain the Confidence to Do This?	58
Breaking Unconscious Biases	59
When Your Perceived Intuition Fails You	60
Coaching Moments: For Yourself and Those You Serve	61
3 Key Takeaways	63

▶ Key 4

High Expectations, High Support	65
Response to Feedback	66
Set a Realistic, High Bar for Yourself	67
Underperforming Leadership	68
What Message Are You Sending?	70
Showing Care and Boundaries	72
Tough Love	73
Mentoring the Mentor	75
Stop Walking on Your Tiptoes	77
3 Key Takeaways	78

▶ Key 5

Be the Calm in the Storm	81
Introduction	81
Fences of Familiarity	83
Beware of Fear-Mongering	84
The Thing about Storms	85
The Storm Inside You	86
The Pressures We Face	89
Who Is Your Shoulder to Lean on?	90
Boundaries Are Not a Bad Word	91
Normalize Caring for You	95
3 Key Takeaways	96

▶ Key 6

Stay on Your Path	99
Introduction	99
The Wrong Path for You	101
No Quick Fixes	102
Self-Reflection as an Art Form	104
Invest in Yourself	106
Think in Shorter Bursts	109
What Is Wrong with Being Confident?	112
Just Be You	113
3 Key Takeaways	113

▶ Key 7

Live in the Present, Visualize the Future	115
Introduction	115
The Dedication of SAS	116
Visualization Is Key	117
Your Circle of Influence	119
Have the Confidence to Do What Is Necessary	120
Self-Love Is Your Strength	122
What Will Set Your School Apart?	123
3 Key Takeaways	124

Meet the Author

▶ **Dr. Kara Knight, Ed.D.,** is an award-winning educator, national speaker, and current Elementary Principal at Boone Trail Elementary in Missouri. Through being the author of two books, *The Confident School Leader* and *Unleash Your Talent*, Kara uses her student-centered leadership approach to help evolve other schools, educators, and leaders in the nation.

Prior to becoming a Principal, Kara was an Assistant Principal, Mentor Teacher/Technology Integrationist, and a teacher. She believes that as a leader you must embody the teacher's heart first and foremost. Kara has also taken many district roles over the years, such as Curriculum Coordinator and Developer, Team Leader, and Equity Team Member. She believes in diving into new experiences and passions to be the most well-rounded leader you can be.

Kara is married to her husband, Stephen. They are expecting their first child in January of 2021!

Acknowledgments

To my family—I love you more than life itself.

To the best Mom in the world, I will always be your favorite—and only daughter. I thank God for you each day.

To the love of my life, Stephen. Everyone deserves to be loved in the way that you love me. I adore you.

My heartfelt appreciation goes to my students. You have shaped and inspired me every step of the way. I pray that you will always be confident in who you are, even if the world does not understand you.

Lastly, to everyone who is reading this book now. My deepest wish is that through these pages you feel heard, validated, and empowered. You are worthy of love and walking in your purpose. Walk confidently forward in your journey of leadership.

Introduction

This is the book I wish I had read ten years ago.

Although I have always seemed confident, confidence is an area that I internally struggled with for years. What other people thought of me ruled supreme in many areas of my life. So much so that it often got in the way of the person I was or wanted to be.

I was self-conscious about my appearance, height, age, womanhood, leadership style, and personality. I seemed secure on the outside, but on the inside I was not. I was adjusting myself based on what I thought society and those around me wanted. I always felt I had to minimize or shelter who I was on behalf of others' comfort. That is not a way to live or lead.

It seems that many others struggle in the same area. Recently, I presented at a digital conference to almost 100 educators. I asked the attendees, "What is one barrier that is getting in your way the most?" Many people responded in the chat with words such as:

- Confidence
- Self-doubt
- My inner critic
- Lack of self-trust

Seeing these words in the chat confirmed that I am on the right path with this book. We all struggle with this in one way or another.

We often point to outside factors for being what is getting in our way, but more than often our self is the most powerful and most dynamic obstacle of all. Our thoughts have more power over us than we often realize. As school leaders, we must make conscious efforts to be mindful and present with our thoughts and beliefs since we are continually navigating the ideas of many around us.

I have continually fought against my inner critic to break barriers as a young leader. One of my main goals is to influence school systems to grow and evolve, including the people we serve. I am a current Elementary School Principal who has done so much to get to this point. If I can, you can too! Before being a Principal, I have always dabbled in many school roles to be the best leader possible. Some of these roles, I also did simultaneously:

- New Teacher District Facilitator
- English Language Arts (ELA) Department Lead
- Social Studies Content Developer
- Mentor Technology Teacher
- Assistant Principal

I believe that to influence others you need to believe in yourself. You also need to dive into as many experiences around you to be as well-rounded as possible. Experiences give you a new perspective. Perspective gives you confidence.

Confidence for me has not grown in a day, month, or year. Trust in myself continues to grow over time, through intentional focus. No matter where you are today, confidence can and will grow in you if you allow it to do so.

This book is not meant to be a handbook on how to be confident or how to fake it until you make it. That strategy will work only for some time. Instead, this book's vision is to awaken the confidence within and validate the leader you already are while pushing you to new heights. My hope is that through these pages you will begin to hear and trust your inner voice to be the leader your students desperately need.

This book is based on 7 keys I developed to influence and implement change as a confident school leader. With the seven chapters of this book, you will dive into one new key to expand upon your leadership per chapter:

- Key 1: Lead with Authenticity
- Key 2: Understand Your Influence
- Key 3: Trust Your Gut
- Key 4: High Expectations, High Support
- Key 5: Be the Calm in the Storm
- Key 6: Stay on Your Path
- Key 7: Live in the Present, Visualize the Future

Within each chapter you will notice the following special features for the busy and eager school leader:

- At the start of each chapter, there is a "Before You Start Reading" box to help unpack what you will learn, while helping your brain quickly digest the new pieces of information
- Research that pairs with many of the book's ideas
- Personal anecdotes from my continued leadership journey
- Reoccurring text boxes in each chapter to feature key strategies to implement now titled "The Confident School Leader" and "Influence & Implement"
- At the end of each chapter, there are 3 Key Takeaways, where I synthesize the 3 most important points of each chapter.

As you read through this book, you will notice that I believe in learning from other lines of work: the business world, start-ups, the health field, the police force, findings from other countries, and beyond. Within this book, leadership research from many sectors is embedded to help us expand your learning, to make new connections, and to break biases.

Take what fills your soul and reject what does not.

This book represents my soul, heart, and continued journey as a current and developing school leader. I hope that you find a friend in me. We are all on different paths as school leaders, but one thing is for sure—we are often navigating a fulfilling but rocky journey in pushing through the politics, fixed beliefs, and stuck mindsets to do what is best for all of our students.

The confidence within your values, beliefs, and mission for students will be the catalyst to influence those around you. Your students and your community need you and what you have to offer, not what you wish you could be.

Within this book are the keys to unlock your influence and to implement change.

Keep loving those around you while doing the difficult and necessary things to do what is mission-critical for your students.

Let us reach new heights and find the confidence within.

Lead with Authenticity

> **BEFORE YOU START READING**
>
> Within this chapter, you will unpack:
> - What it truly means to be a confident school leader
> - Breaking the barriers of what authenticity looks like
> - Continuously creating & reworking your personal vision to inspire you
> - Leading with passion and strengths, while limiting stress around you
> - How to grow into the leader you hope to be

Schools desperately need authentic leaders: People who are unafraid and unapologetically themselves. Leaders who are confident in who they are and who trust themselves. Leaders who forge different paths that fearlessly represent their morals, values, and originality.

We desperately need more leaders who keep it real. Leaders who are in tune with who they are and what they bring to the table. I believe wholeheartedly that you are more likely to serve those around you if you are in tune with yourself.

My Mom was and is the ideal representation of being true to you. She is unable to fake her authenticity. As a high schooler,

I was often shocked by my Mom's ability to know everyone, everywhere. It did not matter if we went to Target, Taco Bell, or the nearest grocery store, she would strike up a conversation with anyone. Patience has never been my strongest trait. So, waiting for her to finish her conversations with everyone in the community was about all I could take. In true "The Biggest High Schoolers Nightmare" fashion, sometimes my Mom would dance in the aisles or sing when we were shopping.

She would strut along, laugh as she sang, and would say "C'mon, Kara!"

I feared the day I would run into any of my crushes as this was going on.

My Mom was also one of our High School secretaries, so I got to see her every day. She was practically famous at my school! All of my friends and classmates would go out of their way to stop by her office. My Mom would give kiddos snacks who did not have anything to eat and would tell students to make sure they were "keeping it real," as she gestured peace signs.

It was not until I was older that I realized how silly it was for me to be embarrassed. My Mom was, and still is, being true to herself, and people love her for it.

Each experience I have in life reinforces the idea that we cannot be anyone less than who we are. Despite what society or people may say, we should never feel the need to shelter or suppress ourselves.

It takes courage to be yourself. It has taken me many years to figure out who I am, and I am still figuring it out and making peace with my imperfections.

In a world that is often edited. Be yourself.

▶ LET AUTHENTICITY LEAD THE WAY

> ❝Students need leaders who look like them, act like them, and dream like them to see the role model they aspire to be. Teachers and staff need this, too.❞

That's a tall order, correct? Yes, but necessary.

When you become a leader, it is an unspoken understanding that you were chosen for the position because those who interviewed you believed that you could lead their school, district, and community. They would not have hired you otherwise. The interview panel believed in your mission, felt that you were a leader they would want to follow, and somehow felt connected to you.

When you find out that you, yes, were chosen for the leadership position, you probably felt a myriad of feelings: grateful, thrilled beyond belief, valued, and scared to death, all at the same time. This is normal. We, as leaders, want to feel that we will make a difference. We want the schools that we lead to have this belief in us as well.

As leaders, we hope what we have to offer is enough for our students, staff, and our community. Deep down, all leaders both worry about and crave being good enough. Even if a person seems flawless, they have inner conflicts as well. Even on our best days, we can still get in the comparison trap.

When you become a leader of any title, these insecurities can be maximized. The worst culprit is often your inner critic.

Just because you are a school leader now does not mean you are suddenly inhuman and lose your feelings, vulnerabilities, and emotions. You are still who you are, but your feelings and vulnerabilities can become magnified when the spotlight is on you, and you become the face of the school, community, and district.

It is a huge responsibility.

When I found out that I would be the next Principal of my elementary school, I was at a loss for words. I was genuinely speechless. I could not believe that the teachers, superintendents, and interview panel felt that I would be good enough to lead them. I was in utter disbelief that I was the individual chosen. There must have been countless other strong leaders out of the candidate pool, right? Why was I chosen? What did they see in me?

All of these unspoken thoughts flooded into my head like a tidal wave while I was offered the position. I remember that my first words were, "Wow, Thank you! I am speechless and incredibly grateful—and yes, I accept!"

My future superintendents must have read my mind at that moment because they said these words I would never forget: "We hired you because of your positivity, energy, and what you bring to the table. Learn to channel that energy. Be yourself. If you lead in any other way, it will not work."

Wow. Yet again, I was speechless.

I felt that I was the Karate Kid being served the truth by the wise Mr. Miyagi himself.

These words of truth spoken over me as I embarked upon my lead principalship journey have been some of the best nuggets of wisdom I have ever heard as a leader.

> **"** Confidence is not having all the answers. It is also not having an ego or being full of yourself. Confidence, instead, is knowing that you have what it takes in all circumstances, every day, all the time. Confidence is the belief that you bring to your soul and every space you enter. **"**

Of course, these items above do not just magically get bestowed over you in true Hogwarts fashion. You will not gain a high level of the above characteristics by wishing for it, dreaming about it, or reading this book alone. You will not become confident suddenly when you accept a leadership position. It is not an instant process. Instead, it is an oscillating process of ups and downs, pivots, dips, and growths. You must have the desire to evolve and the humbleness to know that you are human.

You have to be willing to let authenticity lead the way.

Like a seed, you must water and grow in confidence regularly. As you grow, you will need to foster your ability to adapt. Growing never happens without a cost.

> **"** There is a difference between adapting to others and sacrificing the best of you. Stay focused on your authenticity and the ability to make the mission a reality. Do not sacrifice who you are in the name of leadership. **"**

Along the way, as you grow, I urge you to never trade your authenticity for approval. This will be among the most significant challenges you will face as a leader. Grow in the

---

CONFIDENT SCHOOL LEADERS

If we are going to lead a school, we need to ensure that we have a high level of:

- Character and values
- Self-assuredness in who we are
- Belief in ourselves
- Faith that we can get the job done

self-knowledge that is buried deep within you, so you can step further into your leadership.

As you lead yourself and others, consistently make transparent decisions that go in line with your values. Do not settle for anything less, ever.

▶ LEADERS LEAD THEMSELVES FIRST

Would you ask a student to teach his seatmate two-digit addition without first understanding how to problem-solve similar problems himself? Would you ask a teacher to lead professional development for your staff on a subject that they have no interest or experience in? Would you attempt to run a marathon without first mastering running a mile, 5K, 10K, or half marathon?

If I had to guess, I would say that you answered a loud and resounding no to all of the questions above.

If we apply this same thought process to ourselves, I will ask you this: How can you lead a group of people if you are not proficient at leading yourself?

Let me take it a step further. How can you also build a school culture rooted in values, if the staff members you serve do not know what you stand for?

So, let me honestly ask: Do you feel that you are currently stepping forward and leading yourself as a person?

When I ask you this question, I urge you to think beyond the field of education. Just as I believe that you cannot lead others without leading yourself, I also believe that if you lead yourself well on a day-to-day at home, you will again thrive in how you show up for others at work.

As we go deeper, stay in tune with the fact that all people show you their values and belief systems, whether they realize it or not. Your actions will always show the kind of leader you are before your words will. Integrity is seen and heard, not told.

What kind of message are you sending about your leadership?

Leadership is not built through the most significant or monument actions, although that helps. Just like trust, leadership is created by every little interaction you have, day after day.

▶ CREATING A PERSONAL VISION

Think about the best or one of the best days you had as a leader. A day when you were genuinely walking into your purpose. A day that you left your school or building feeling confident that you made a meaningful impact. A day that you knew in your heart of hearts that you were influencing change.

- What precisely happened, and how did you truly live your best life that day?
- What did you see, hear, and experience as an individual?
- How did those around you react?

When I think about my best days as a leader, the memories are always tied with how I was doing what I do best. Not the areas I wish I did best in, the areas where I flourish more naturally.

When I walk in my purpose, I know I will have a great and memorable day with students and staff. When I am in tune with who I am, my feelings, and those around me, I know I will make an impact. When I know my own path, I will be more likely to conquer the day.

When I am confident with myself, I know that I can be a ray of light for others who need some vitamin D in their lives.

On the other hand, when I go through the motions and do what others want, I know that I will leave work feeling depleted. I know in those moments I will feel deprived of what I stand for. Those moments of failure as a leader have taught me the on-the-job experience I needed. The hurts stung at the moment but left me wanting to improve.

Every time I mess up, I realize I am human. We cannot do it entirely right at all times, but we can keep the confidence in our journey of self-growth. No one can take that away from you, only yourself.

We will have highs and lows as a leader; this I know for sure. We will have moments where we encounter crises that make our hearts sink. We will make or watch others make mistakes that make us question if leadership is the right place for us. If this has crossed your mind before, do not feel alone.

Yet always keep in mind that we will see the most incredible life-giving moments if we take the time to step back and notice with a kinder eye.

As I write this, I am currently leading in the pandemic that we all know so well, COVID-19. I never thought when I accepted my head principal job in December of 2019 that the world would change dramatically by the time I started my first year as the school leader. Thank goodness I at least had leadership and assistant principal leadership experience under my belt.

In March of 2020 in the United States, within a matter of days, leaders, teachers, technology staff members, central office administration had been tasked with helping students lead, learn, and stay well fed during an international crisis. There is no roadmap or book on how to properly do this.

Although there is not a list of hard and fast things we need to do as leaders during unexpected times, one thing is for sure: We need to be able to count on ourselves, our abilities, and the internal strength that is rooted within us.

Whether it is COVID-19 or any crisis that emerges, let our experiences push us to growth and evolution, rather than fear and scarcity.

Believe. In. Yourself.

Any observer knows that a crisis will show the real skills, confidence, and belief system, whether we asked for it or not.

> ❝Rather than saying, "I cannot believe I am leading during such a time as this!" Ask yourself, "How can I use my leadership abilities to make the greatest influence during this time?"❞

Wisdom and expertise are important; yet they do not correlate the wisdom with either a job title or number of years. Experience does not necessarily translate to a number of years. Instead, experiences and learning require the motivation to constantly be one of the hardest workers and learners in any setting or in any season of life.

Whether you are a student who is breaking boundaries as a sophomore, a new school leader, or a veteran superintendent, people will not admire you by what you know. They will admire for how you inspire them to grow.

▶ UNEXPECTED TIMES CAN DELIVER EXCELLENCE

Even through these uncharted times, we see leaders and educators putting their best foot forward and showing the world what they got! We have teachers driving by students' homes for their birthdays to see smiles on their faces. We have technology directors who are delivering Wi-Fi hotspots to students' families and distributing supplies to our students. We have cafeteria staff who are spending hours, bagging hundreds of food bags each day to keep our students' stomachs full.

Leaders are those who step into the unknown with the firm belief that they can make a difference. It does not take a role, a title, or a special recognition to become a leader. It takes a will and belief to use your influence for good, paired with the determination to build your skill set.

Case in point—Leaders lead.

Leaders do not always choose what situation they are leading others through, but they can decide how they will use their influence to get their team through the rough waters.

Neither you or I wanted COVID-19. No one wants this for our communities, kids, and families.

We do want resilience and confidence for all, and it can begin with you and I.

Throughout the ebbs and flows of what we do, we need to stay focused on what drives us.

What drives you? What issue in education or the world are you aiming to improve? We are all passionate about kids, but what is your divine specialty?

You may be passionate about equity, social justice, Project Based Learning (PBL), counseling, facilities, social work, fostering health and fitness, building student leaders, and more. What areas make your heart sing?

We need to truly become one with our vision to live it and share it with others.

Which leads me to this question: What is your vision and mission for your life?

Over the years, I have created many personal mission statements, and after a couple of months, or sooner, I can sometimes feel uninspired by my creations. That is normal, and whenever we outgrow our mission, it is time to dream bigger and create.

▶ YOUR VISION

But last year I created a personal statement that states, "Do what moves you." When I read this, I am reminded to walk in my purpose. Through this statement, I am reminded that I have only one life, and I need to act like it.

As I make decisions or as I speak, I often think to myself:

- Does this move me?
- Does this represent me?
- Does this show the person I am and the person I want to be?
- Does this inspire me?

Changes are made not from giant steps forward or by accomplishing huge events. Instead, real change is made on a visceral level. Change becomes innate in us if we begin to let ourselves change with every little decision and interaction we make every day. Changes happen when small events occur repeatedly.

Continuous little changes, rather than a few significant changes, will make the biggest impact—every single time.

I am a visual person. Many people are. Although it is helpful to have my mission statement written out, as I shared earlier, I have to be honest and tell you another strategy that helps me best.

I have created a bimonthly vision board/action plan.

Some people develop a vision board to stay grounded in their future, while others write up a detailed action plan. I like to do both together.

I am not an artist by any means; although I to pretend to be one with my watercolor art, I love to sketch and doodle to get my point across and express myself.

I believe that that you can stay grounded and then execute your mission if you can:

- Remind yourself of your goals as much as possible
- Make your thinking visible
- Have exact daily steps to make it happen

To do this, as I mentioned, I create a new vision board every two months. Two months is my sweet spot. For me personally, if I keep the timeline too long for my action plan, it loses its luster for me. I stop caring about it. But, if I keep the vision in bite-size pieces that still have a little substance in length, I meet my point of impact.

To give you an idea, my vision board has nine spots where I doodle the nine things I will do every single day to live in my mission. They are not all school-related, and many of my goals are more focused to me as a human. But, by focusing on self-development, I will most definitely see school improvement occur as a result. Any change in your life will affect every area of your life.

When leaders shape their behavior, it changes their school, whether intentional or not.

To be transparent, here are a couple of the items on my action plan that I drew through pictures, not words:

- Be creative
- Call family every day
- Get closer to God

My action steps show my purpose. They display my mission. Through reading just three out of my nine action plan items, you can see that I value art as a creative release. You may notice that family is a massive part of my life. You may also see that my relationship with God is pivotal, as well.

Although these are personal goals, I believe it is essential to understand the connection between personal success and professional success. Leading others well includes a motivation to improve schools and to love people. Leading yourself requires the same approach, a catalyst to improve yourself while loving yourself every step of the way. As you continue your leadership journey, stay grounded with who you are now and who you want to evolve to be.

▶ QUESTIONS FOR REFLECTION

- Do you have a current vision for yourself in your life or life as a leader?
- If you do not yet have a vision, how can you create a vision that holds deep meaning for you? How will you make it visible so you will be continuously exposed to it?

- If you have a vision, can it be tweaked or adjusted to hold more power in your life?
- If you are a school leader, how will you share your vision with others? How can you inspire those you serve to follow your lead?

Someone's wild imagination does not create leaders. Leaders are created by someone, somewhere putting in the work to make their vision in their mind the reality that they come to see. Only you can create the leader you aspire to be!

▶ DASHES OF HONESTY

Leading yourself begins with being comfortable enough to give yourself a personal truth that may pierce your heart at times.

As the age-old saying correctly expresses—No one is perfect.

Even the person you most look up to in your life has major vital areas to grow upon in their lives. Case in point: Let's do an activity.

Get out a piece of paper and a pencil. Go ahead and list everything you think you need to be a perfect leader. Write these characteristics down and take a look at what comes to your mind as fast as you can.

Ready, set, GO!

Now, after finishing your little writing assignment, I want you to re-read your list and take a long hard look at what you wrote down from top to bottom. After reading all of these characteristics, is there anyone you know who embodies everything that you wrote?

If you know this said perfect person, pick up the phone right now and thank them for being a fictional fairytale character straight from fantasyland.

Most likely, this imaginary person does not exist. That is okay.

What is my point?

The truth is our lists run bigger in our heads than we often realize. We think if we could only do x, y, and z, we would be a better leader in our heads. We think that we have more weaknesses than the next person. We struggle to realize that we can still be a leader who is flawed.

Each person will always have room to grow.

Everyone is human, and no one is immune to making mistakes. What is most important is being able to stay grounded between these two sides of thought:

1. Be proud of the work that you have done
2. You will always have room to grow

As an educator and leader, it can be tough to acknowledge both of these points while not getting stuck in your head between either point of view.

If you stay too focused on the mindset that you need to improve, you will become your worst self-critic without being proud of your growth journey. On the other hand, if you think everything you are doing is grand, your ego will dominate you and inhibit you from continuing to learn without noticing your areas of weakness.

> **❝** The difference between those who continually evolve and those who do not is transparency with oneself. Transparency, paired with discipline for self-evolution, creates an unstoppable leader.
> Who doesn't want to feel unstoppable? **❞**

Where would you say you are between both points of views I mentioned above? Do you stay somewhere in the middle? Do you gravitate toward one side or the other? Do you make an intentional effort to embrace both perspectives? How do you catch and bounce back when you feel yourself jumping into negative land?

We need to give ourselves the dashes of honesty to put ourselves back to reality. Early on in my educational journey, I learned that although I am excited to know everything I possibly can soak in, I could not possibly find all the knowledge out there. I will never be an expert. That is a tough pill to swallow sometimes, but it motivates me to keep going, to keep learning.

On the other side of that token, I will be the first to admit that I struggle with being too hard on myself. I will reflect to the degree where reflection becomes self-sabotage. Rather than noticing anything that I do well, I will wish that I did 101 things differently and not honor the process or the joy in a moment. Over time, I have learned that this is not healthy.

Self-reflection is hard like that—You find the areas you need to grow upon, and they will hit you smack dab in the face.

▶ BUILDING ON SHIFTING ROCK

It is so ingrained in us to always evolve that we sometimes struggle with being present and happy in the here and now. This is also illustrated in a study that Harvard research depicted through a workforce consulting firm titled "Life Meets Work" (Levin, 2018). The study surveyed over 1,000 college-educated employees who were asked for their own work experience and how their leader handles stress. It was also measured how their leaders' stress affects others in the workplace.

According to the study, "Only 7 percent of employees surveyed believe that their stressed leaders effectively lead their teams, and only 11 percent of employees with stressed leaders are highly engaged at work (Levin, 2018)." It is also important to note that if the workforce believed that leaders struggled to manage their stress in a healthy way, it affected the perception of the leader. For example, leaders with minimal coping skills had more than 50 percent of their staff see their leaders as ineffective or detrimental to the team (Levin, 2018).

With that said, when our employees view us in this way, this will lessen their ability to bring their best selves and stay motivated. This study helps to further reinforce the importance of aligning ourselves with our emotions, characters, and values. If we need help and mentorship, it is crucial we seek it out. Remember, authenticity is key, and you will know best if you are living a "less than who you are" life.

In addition to this research, there are also fascinating finds from Gallup studies in Japan. The study began in 2017 after the Japanese government published data that showed that over 20 percent of Japanese employees were at a higher risk of death due to being overworked (Jim Asplund, 2020). In Japan, they refer to this as karoshi. This study gained information from nearly 2,500 Japanese employees and found that high stress was linked to excessively long work weeks (Jim Asplund, 2020). As leaders, we understand the demands of long work weeks and how that can affect us. Therefore, this may not be new information to you.

Even more impressive than this was the fact that Gallup further dissected the information to determine the relationship to

> **INFLUENCE & IMPLEMENT:**
>
> Successful leaders are able to:
>
> - Walk in their purpose
> - Have engagement & enthusiasm for their work
> - Use their natural strengths to achieve high performance
> - Find moments to take care of themselves to nourish your wellbeing

stress to these three areas: employee engagement and enthusiasm for their work, strengths, and how individuals used their strengths to achieve high performance, and wellbeing about a person's life.

(Jim Asplund, 2020)

> ❝The research found that employees who enjoyed what they did for work, who focused on their wellbeing elements, and who worked in workplace environments that fought for their natural strengths were significantly less likely to suffer from high stress.❞

Each individual is responsible to a vast degree for their wellbeing. Yet, at the same time, an employer and leader are also responsible for supporting an individual that works within their school and organization. The same can be said for a leader leading themselves and their own life. If a leader is not actively engaged in their work and passionate about what they are doing, the likelihood that their stress will grow is very high.

Our ability to create environments where both the leader and those they serve can thrive is an essential piece of the puzzle. We often talk about supporting those we serve but forget that we need to take care of ourselves as leaders, too. The leader sets the tone for everything. Therefore, what message are you sending by the status of your passion for your work and your wellbeing?

Homes cannot be built on a shifting, rocky, or sliding foundation. For example, when a potential homeowner is interested in building their home on a mountain, the contractors and construction team cannot develop and drop the house down on the rock. No one wants their home to slide down the cliff! Therefore, teams work to meticulously engineer a new foundation so that both the mountain and home can withstand the different environmental and gravity factors. Excessive concrete is used, rocks around the area are cut or cleared, and advanced technology is used to get the job done. It is an extensive project to build a foundation that will last.

So, why in the world am I going on a rock tangent? First of all, it is interesting. Also, this particular example sounds familiar to leadership sometimes. We do not always walk into situations within education where the strong prebuilt foundations already established. That's where we can come in as a leader!

Leaders do not just show up when things are going well, they show up when they are needed.

If your foundation of leadership skills and experience has been lackluster, there is always a way to create new and better experiences. You need the work ethic, belief system, and pure patience to make it happen.

Maybe your current school is struggling in several areas and you feel that there are many items you need to focus on. Perhaps you do not know where to start? That's okay. Messy is often looked upon with grunts, sighs, or judgment. The truth is messy is a beautiful thing. Messy provides an ultimate starting point for radical growth. But, just like building a sturdy house on shifting rock, you must be willing to think outside of the cookie-cutter box and put in the concrete work. Nothing can substitute pure passion and hard work. Nothing. My Mom has always said, "Anything worth doing is worth doing well."

> **"** Leaders lead themselves well to lead others well. Our mindfulness, or lack thereof, can leave those around us with a feeling of being unsettled or misguided. It is okay to show vulnerabilities, but if your energy is demonstrated from a place of consistent high stress, you will lose the belief in those around you. **"**

I cannot say this enough: To create the foundation that you need to withstand the wind, shifts, and storms. Don't start by asking others to do the tough stuff. Start with yourself.

Without a shadow of a doubt, we know that our subconscious thoughts and behaviors will rub off on our staff and students in some shape or form. Therefore, be honest with yourself and your journey to continually grow personally, so it is shown professionally.

If you sugarcoat things in your mind, how will you be able to hear the truth when and if it comes from someone else? Do not wait for others to lead you. Become the leader you need for yourself.

▶ TRUE AUTHENTICITY

Managing your authenticity is one of the most challenging journeys we have as leaders.

As Rob Goffee and Gareth Jones state in a *Harvard Business Review* article titled "Managing Authenticity, The Paradox of Great Leadership," no leader can look into a mirror and say, "I am authentic. A person cannot be authentic on his or her own (Goffee and Jones, 2014)."

In other words, if you are authentic or not will mostly be decided by those around you, but I believe that in each of us if we look inside and listen to our internal compass, we know if we are true to who we are, or not.

Sometimes we need a push, a nudge, or need to be shouldered along by those around us, but most of this work should be led by you. Leaders lead those around them—and themselves.

We are walking knees deep in the social media age where filters are the normal thing to add to every picture. Even the images that we do post without photo editing are added with the #nofilter hashtag. We do this with a sense of pride for being brave enough to show our wrinkles and imperfections. Some pictures we post have numerous filters layered on top of themselves, and we do not even look recognizable to ourselves and others. We can post this image of what we envision ourselves to look like in our heads or what we hope to look like. In our minds, this can be easier than posting the real thing.

I have fallen victim to the same examples that I mentioned above. I think we all have. What are we afraid of? Sometimes, it is hard to be confident when you feel you need to be perfect.

Undoubtedly, this social media way of being has trickled into all areas of our lives. This is part of the reason why Brené Brown's work on vulnerability has taken off and been vital to many of us. Brené Brown is a researcher and licensed social worker who studies human connection. Her first TED talk, titled "The Power of Vulnerability," has over 47 million views and counting at this time. Within this TED talk, Brown (2010), shares this,

> When we work from a place that says, "I'm enough," then we stop screaming and start listening. We're kinder and gentler to the people around us, and we're kinder and gentler to ourselves."

It is clear that people seek refuge within her message of vulnerability and seek excellence, not perfection. When we know who we are and we lead from that place, people will notice and be better as a result.

As leaders, vulnerability breeds authenticity. Then, authenticity builds confident leadership.

As mentioned at the beginning of this chapter, to lead oneself it is essential to name and be aware of your:

- Character and values
- Personal mission
- Goals
- Belief to make it happen

▶ NEVER PERFECT, ALWAYS AUTHENTIC

These four ideas above are the base point of authentic leadership. Being authentic means that we must know who we are and be true to ourselves. This is a lifelong journey that can adapt and change directions during different stages of our leadership journey. We must have a strong base point on who we are and what we stand for. This base point can be a beautiful foundation that will be grown upon as you continue to throw yourself into new experiences.

But, if you are a newer leader to the scene like myself, I encourage you to feel empowered in who you are. Do not think that because you may lack experience, you lack wisdom. Although I know I have an abundant amount to continue to learn, it is vital to keep in mind that I was chosen for my position because both my supervisors and my staff believe in me to lead them. If they believe in me to lead them, I must first believe in myself.

Reader, I feel empowered to write this book because I am currently walking this journey beside you. You are not alone. We are diving into this thing called leadership together!

This school year is my fourth year in administration and my first year as a Head Principal. For years, becoming a Principal has been a goal and a lifelong dream for me. Now that my vision is becoming my reality, I would be lying if I said that there was not a little fear that my failures as a leader will exceed what I can bring to the table.

If you reach your goals and start sensing fear, feel relief because this is a normal visceral reaction. Even Adele and Rihanna still have stage fright when they are about to approach the stage—it must be true because I read it online.

Whether you are a leader newer to the scene or not, if you ever feel fear creeping in when you are about to take the next jump, step back and remind yourself what has gotten you this far already. Reflect on all of your hours diving into professional development to expand yourself. Think of all the books you read personally or within a book club to push your mindset—Mull over all of the collaborations you have had with your colleagues to build connections and learning. Contemplate the hours you spent becoming your own mentor and questioning your values, goals, and missions.

Do you still have room to grow? Most definitely.

But give yourself credit for how far you have already come. Then, check yourself at the door when your actions and your mission do not match. Be your own best critic, supporter, and advocate.

Remember this: You are enough. You are the person for the job. You were called to lead your school and community. Your hours behind the scenes that no one saw has mentally prepared you for this moment. Breathe in confidence and radiate authenticity. If you don't trust yourself, how can others?

One of my newer mantras has been: I will never be perfect, but I can always be authentic.

I know that I will second-guess myself and make mistakes. Who doesn't? None of us are immune to this. I can own my mistakes, knowing I am doing the best I can.

I can step in my truth as a leader and know that my motivations are good-hearted, my intentions are pure, and that I am working my tail off behind the scenes. All the while, even through my shortcomings, I know that I am getting closer to the leader that I want to be each day as a leader.

If I am authentic, a day in a life in leadership looks like this for me: a mix between focus and play. When I am in the zone, I am in the zone. I have my leadership game face on and crave efficiency and using time wisely. I am the person at meetings who walks in over-prepared, ready to take detailed notes and help the flow of the conversation come along. At the same time,

I love to have fun and make others laugh. You can catch me in the hallways laughing with students, singing songs on the spot to motivate them, and attempting dance moves that bring me back to my glory days as a dancer.

In a snapshot, that is me—a driven, goofy, silly, but exceptionally dedicated person.

What does an authentic day of leadership look like to you?

Don't stop until you are proud of your soul.

If you are not proud of who you are and how you represent yourself today, tomorrow is another shot to try again. You do not have to wait until another season of life or New Year's Eve to reevaluate yourself. Start as you are reading this book.

> **❝** Each day do all you can to be intentional with everything you do. If you remain true to yourself along the way, you will not only make a difference within your school, but you will make yourself proud. We often talk about making an impact on others, but how often do we talk about being happy with who we are? **❞**

▶ ARE YOU GROWING TO THE LEADER YOU WISH TO BE?

As a leader, one of the worst feelings is making a decision that is not in line with your values, vision, and goals. You may not even realize the impact of your decision at the moment, but you eventually will. Maybe you did not know all of the factors at play before making the decision. Perhaps you felt pressure from others. Perhaps you made a quick choice to please those around you. Either way, mistakes that do not align with your vision will leave a mark on your heart. My hope is that these experiences push you to do better.

When this happens, do not allow your anxieties or insecurities to take root in you. Instead,

> **❝** If any decision you made did not make you proud, it is time to realign and regroup with your character, values, mission, and what inspired you to lead in the first place. **❞**

When I think of authentic leaders, I think of those willing to admit they have room to grow. Many of these leaders do not wait to hear feedback from others. They will begin the reflections themselves, way before they even ask other staff members what they think. By their actions, you can tell that they are reflecting on a personal level to evolve and adapt their practice day after day. They are confident in who they are and are motivated enough to make the magic happen!

This level of realness in leadership inspires others to lean in closer to who they are.

If you see your leader modeling the way and showing it can be done, it pushes others watching to step up their game. You level up the playing field with excellence.

But, if you see a disjointed leader who is expecting more from others than they are from themselves, you will quickly lose respect and potentially the willpower to grow. Never exchange your values for the approval of others. Be confidently you.

Above all, lean into your mission, name it, own it, shine a huge spotlight on it! Authenticity breeds authenticity.

Are you growing into the type of leader who says and does the things you believe?

▶ 3 KEY TAKEAWAYS

- All people show you their values and belief systems, whether they realize it or not. Your actions will always show the kind of leader you are before your words ever will. Be in tune with your feelings, motives, and steps to lean in closer to who you want to be.
- Build and name your vision for your leadership. Ensure that your vision is rooted in a belief to make it happen with the character and values that you stand for. You cannot lead others if you do not first succeed at leading yourself. If you are starting from a rocky place, know that you can build a strong foundation. You need to be successful in even the messiest situations.
- You will never be perfect, but you can always be authentic. Each day, you should be getting closer and closer to the leader you aim to be. If you fall short of this, be willing, to be honest with yourself and get ready to realign and regroup.

References

Brown, B., (2010, June). The power of vulnerability. Retrieved January 02, 2021, from https://www.ted.com/talks/brene_brown_the_power_of_vulnerability?language=en

Goffee, R., & Jones, G. (2014, August 01). Managing authenticity: The paradox of great leadership. Retrieved January 02, 2021, from https://hbr.org/2005/12/managing-authenticity-the-paradox-of-great-leadership

Jim Asplund, M. (2020, December 11). How strengths, wellbeing and engagement reduce burnout. Retrieved January 02, 2021, from https://www.gallup.com/cliftonstrengths/en/312467/strengths-wellbeing-engagement-reduce-burnout.aspx

Levin, M. (2018, February 28). Harvard research reveals how mindful leaders develop better companies and happier employees. Retrieved January 02, 2021, from https://www.inc.com/marissa-levin/harvard-research-reveals-how-mindful-leaders-develop-better-companies-happier-employees.html

Key 2: Understand Your Influence

BEFORE YOU START READING

Within this chapter, you will unpack:

- How to give yourself grace to make mistakes, while rising above them
- What it means to fail well and with commitment
- How to use your unique experiences to create an influence that only you can build
- What to do when you have been overworked to the point of inaction
- How to grow in confidence, even if you wonder how you and your interests will "fit in"

Isn't it wild that you are responsible and accountable to an entire school, student body, and surrounding community as a school leader? Whoa. Before we go further into this chapter, we must not understate this weighty responsibility you have.

When I think about that responsibility, I feel both blessed and then slightly or incredibly overwhelmed, depending on the day.

Does anyone else think about this vast concept as a leader? Or is it just me. I know I cannot be the only one who goes down this deep philosophical rabbit hole in my education thoughts. In all honesty, and seriousness, we are responsible for a lot as leaders—more than we often realize. Most importantly, we are the caretakers of livelihood and education for our students.

With that said, we do not just think about our current students, but we plan for future generations' success. We are always thinking, feeling, and planning.

> **"** There is never a day as a school leader where your impact does not matter. What we do in the here and now will set the trajectory for students in future school years. **"**

In other words, my choices as a leader will directly affect my school community for years to come. This is a humbling thought that I often stir upon.

This magnificent yet sometimes terrifying responsibility starts the second you gain the keys to the metaphorical school castle.

▶ THE KEYS ARE YOURS

As a school leader, you probably will always remember the first time that someone gave you keys to your new building or space. Whether you are an assistant principal, head principal, central office member, or beyond, the feeling stays with you forever.

When the keys land in your hand, you understand how much responsibility and influence you have. When someone gives you these keys, it is a symbolic way to show that you are being entrusted with the building. Not just the physical structure itself, but all of the staff and students who will walk within our halls.

I never take this responsibility lightly.

I bet you feel the same way.

As I write these pages, I need to share my vulnerability, story, and truth.

Some days, I feel like an incredible school leader walking into my purpose and living my best life. Yet, there have been many days where I go home feeling depleted—like I have given every bit of my heart and soul to my school, yet have nothing left to give myself or my family.

Those are the days I often fall asleep on the couch without eating dinner or taking a shower. These are the times where the reality of working endless hours in leadership humbles you. No matter what your nameplate says your role is, you are a human.

These feelings on your worst days can leave you wondering how much of an impact you have made thus far. You wonder: Am I even making a difference?

Isn't it interesting how your mind can play tricks on you? The exhaustion you feel can create a foggy mind. This haziness can fill you with doubt rather than with purpose.

Sometimes it is too easy to share the best moments of our jobs. Do not get me wrong. There is nothing wrong with sharing the positives. I am all about being a force of good. Yet, it crosses into unhealthy territory when you do not allow yourself to feel all the feels. Leaders, including myself, struggle with the pressure to have all things figured out all the time. There is always a reason for our actions, whether we realize it or not. Sometimes we pretend we have it all together to:

- Keep our leadership persona up
- If we lack general support or encouragement
- If we do not want to be a bother to others by asking for support
- If we lack inner confidence
- If we are scared of falling flat on our face

I have fallen victim to feeling all of the fears and points made above. Every single one of them. No shame here or pointing any fingers.

> **"**It is important to note that confidence is not having all the answers. Instead, confidence is knowing yourself well enough to see what you need and to ask for it. **"**

I have to tell you, even though we try so hard not to make a mistake, I truly believe from my experience that confidence grows best when you have failed and failed often.

We often think that failure is a bad word. In education, we all have tried to normalize the name over the years, but there is still a negative connotation, especially as a leader. We often share with our staff and students how vital failing is, but we do not also believe the same can be said for us.

Leaders want their staff and students to make mistakes so they can learn and grow.

But, we often do not give ourselves the same grace to fail and try again when it comes to our position. It is okay for our staff to learn through doing, but not ourselves. We hold ourselves to this standard of impossible perfection.

Where is the logic in that?

I believe we have good intentions; our wires have just become a bit crossed. Many of us are inner perfectionists who hold ourselves to the highest possible standards. We also do not want to be a poor example to our staff. We realize how central our jobs are in the everyday inner workings of a school.

Occasionally, our fears can be amplified if our supervisors support the notion that we have to be on our A-games 24/7. Most of the doubts we have within are self-initiated, while others can be the farmers who plant seeds of uncertainty.

▶ FAILING WITH COMMITMENT

Have you ever heard the phrase "fail fast, learn faster"? As Thomas Watson, Sr., from IBM said, "The fastest way to succeed is to double your failure rate." I believe there is some truth to this.

Our influence grows best through failure. I believe that failure is only built through intentional experiences. For every person. In every role.

No one is immune to failure.

If we are committed to evolving, we should all be failing every day. If we are not failing, are we even pushing the limits of what is possible? Or are we content with the customary?

Moreover, if we ask our staff and students to be comfortable with intentional flops, we need to be the ones to normalize failure.

This idea is inclusive of all leadership roles: superintendents, central office leadership, board members, directors, administrators, assistant principals, and beyond.

When others are making mistakes with the intention of bettering their practice, we must continually praise their efforts.

We must fail with purpose, too, and to add in levels of transparency. Those we serve need to see us learning from our missteps; make your learning visible! There is nothing wrong with leaders showing their humanness. Let's normalize this concept, readers. We are the only ones who can make it happen.

▶ FAILURE-TOLERANT LEADERSHIP

Our influence as a leader is limitless. Everything we do is connected, and it always matters.

With this in mind, here are two statements I feel to my core.

- Even if you have the best intentions to help, you will still mess up
- Our students should always be our #1 reason for continued growth

We have to gain a healthy comfort level in this area as leaders.

Do not be afraid to mess up, because you will again, and again.

Let me tell you this: Your learning from the mess-up is more critical than the mess-up itself. Your failures can be the trajectory to your purpose.

> ❝We as leaders are so scared sometimes to say the wrong thing and to do the wrong thing that we often turn away from the very things we need to do and the conversations we need to have. ❞

Harvard Business Review echoes these thoughts of failure with their coined term of "failure-tolerant leadership." As shared earlier, failing faster is a great starting point. We have to gain a comfort level with our errors and learn from them. This is the journey of learning and leading.

Yet, it does not stop there. You cannot just fail. You must also fail well. On this note, *Harvard Business Review* beautifully states:

> There are failures, and there are failures. Some mistakes are lethal—producing and marketing a dysfunctional car tire, for example. At no time can management be casual about issues of health and safety. But encouraging failure doesn't mean abandoning supervision, quality control, or respect for sound practices. Just the opposite. Managing for failure requires executives to be more engaged, not less.
> (Farson & Keyes, 2002)

In other words, we should not be asking others and ourselves to fail, just to fail. That would be sending the wrong message.

You would never tell someone to make mistakes wildly without any purpose at all. In addition, negligence, inexcusable acts, and repeated acts that show a lack of compassion or respect are not tolerable failures.

▶ INTENTION IS EVERYTHING

Failing with intention looks something like this: We try something different or new to better our practice. We fail or succeed. We pause. We reflect. We learn. We collaborate. We try again.

As a leader, we must take action from our faults and the faults of others. What is the point of failure with a purpose if you do nothing with the experience? Reflect upon this as well: Once you fail, are you using that experience to catapult you and others to greater heights?

I will be honest with you here; you and your staff may:

- Intentionally collaborate on a building goal
- Place your time and resources together
- Dive into professional development

Even with the above efforts, it is possible that you will not see the student growth level you expected. This does not mean that you and your team are a failure.

There is a difference between failing with purpose or merely failing because you did not try. Ask these thoughtful questions and use deep self-reflection to help guide and redirect your team. Make your failures meaningful. Keep planting the seeds, knowing that not every seed will flourish from the harvest; do not ever forget that learning blossoms through the cracks of our well-intentioned mistakes.

▶ YOUR INFLUENCE EFFECT

Everyone has influence, whether they are aware of the magnitude of the influence or not. Influence does not ask you if you want it. Influence is a state of being and doing.

It is important to note that authority does not equal influence. Power does not also equal influence. Power and authority thrive on hierarchy and demands. Influence grows from one's understanding of how their thoughts, emotions, and actions impact others. The quality of your ideas will always trickle down to others.

Your influence effect is most likely more remarkable than what you imagine in your head. The ironic thing about influence is we often do not know where it ends. Yet, we do know where influence begins—with us.

Every single person influences every role and position they are in. This is the case inside and outside of education.

▶ LOOKING INTO THE BUSINESS WORLD

According to Deloitte, a leading global provider of audit and assurance, consulting, financial advisory, risk advisory, tax, and related services, customers on average tell 16 people about a negative experience they had with a brand. On the other hand, if the experience with a brand was positive, customers tell only nine people on average about the experience (McLain, 2018). Research from Deloitte also shows how positive experiences preserve customers for years longer while also encouraging customers to spend more than 140 percent more money on the brand (McLain, 2018).

What can we gather from this business world data?

Influence matters.

The same can be said in education. When our students, staff, and community members are positively engaged, our school culture feels strong, cohesive, and rooted in purpose.

If we feel a lack of engagement in our school community between any or all constituents, we have to ask ourselves why that is.

Like in business, usually, a lack of staff, student, or community engagement is due to poor experiences people have had in the past. I have seen it first-hand. One poor experience with one person in a school community can alter how one feels about the entire school and district.

> **"** Experiences create influence for both the customer and the business. Most of the time, I would venture to say that if someone has either a negative or a positive experience with a brand, it is due to a person-to-person interaction. The brand may be the company, but each person who works for a brand is a walking and talking brand manager in the customer's eyes. **"**

Then, when someone has this poor experience, they are more likely to share it with others on social media. One perceived

> **CONFIDENT SCHOOL LEADERS**
>
> As an influencer: To understand where you are now, you must start with a personal inventory:
>
> - Has your school progressively grown as a result of your influence?
> - How so?
> - What areas of growth still exist?
> - How can you persistently promote progression in each area(s)?

negative experience can affect the way that numerous others see the school as a whole.

We must become aware of the informal clout that each school community member has. This begins with us as leaders. Although we cannot control what others may say and think about us, we can influence the experiences we create.

Leaders who lead with positive influence understand that they influence others and that others also have the opportunity to influence them. Influence can be mutual, or it can be one-sided, in both positive and negative directions.

> ❝The foundation of all relationships is communication. ❞

As you continue to reflect, you will need to build trust and rapport with as many stakeholders as possible. In my opinion,

When people feel that you are accessible, transparent, and want to keep communication fluid and open, they are more willing to have positive experiences with you.

Once you can continually build upon rapports that you have established, you will see your level of influence skyrocket.

The truth of the matter is that when you are an influencer, your job never ends. Your influence will never cease. Therefore, you will always need to reflect on the power of your presence.

Influence means you will need to continue to sustain the bonds you have with others while also building fresh relationships as new students, staff, and community members enter your building.

We must help all things grow, including ourselves, while finding ways to focus on as many elements as you can simultaneously. Everything is connected. We are connected. We can choose to be the influence that breaks boundaries for the better or not. The choice is always ours.

From my own experience of shifting school cultures, you will continually work on yourself to build bonds and help others grow.

▶ SLOW DOWN, WHEN YOU CAN

Have you ever felt as a school leader that everything around you is literally on fire simultaneously? I have. Usually, this type of situation occurs on Fridays or right before, or after a holiday break.

> "You will never be a true connoisseur in one area because each area is always growing. Thus, I urge you to gain confidence in who you are now. You do not need to wait to be a positive influence. Get out there and be that inspiration."

Sometimes, this experience can also meet you when you take over a new building or transition into a different role. Change can often make people uneasy, even if the actions taking place are pushing a school forward.

Leadership can feel full of contradictions. We can be the most optimistic people in the world, while also being a realist. These two states of mind often happen concurrently.

What do I mean by this? Leaders notice and celebrate the good around them while feeling internally overwhelmed by the work that still needs to occur. Being a Principal or Superintendent can feel like being the mayor of your city. You are supporting countless stakeholders with various concerns while ensuring all you do aligns with your vision, mission, values, and campaign slogan.

This is why leadership can feel lonesome. You are the heavy-duty base for the people you serve, day in and day out. While also continually setting goals and processing how to fulfill your action plan.

I call this typical leadership response, the brain strain.

Let me give you a real-life example. I know nothing about cars. I drive an older vehicle because I love the model of my car and its durability. I could care less about having a new car. I also never was interested in learning about how a car functions. We all have our passions, right? Cars and vehicles are not mine.

> "One of the worst feelings as a leader is feeling overwhelmed to the point of inaction."

It is embarrassing to admit this, but I am all about a great metaphor so that I will sacrifice my ego for a good example.

My lack of interest in cars also carries over to being out of touch with my vehicle's daily wear and tear. Often, I overlook glaring signs when my car needs a tune-up. I will ride my vehicle for too long on a "Check Engine" light or wait to fill my tank with gas until it is eerily close to the "E."

Since my car is older, I seriously have to stop doing both of those things. A check engine light could be trying to tell me that my car needs new oil or that there are other significant needs to address. As we know, oil changes are crucial routines that help reduce and remove excess dirt that builds up over time. The benefits do not end with cleanliness. Fresh oil can help with engine efficiency and improving your car's gas mileage. That all sounds fantastic, correct?

Of course!

The issue is that if I proactively take my car to the shop, it requires me to do many things outside my regular routine that interfere with my day-to-day. Most of all, it takes up time I do not have. Plus, who wants to go to get their car fixed? Each time you leave with a bill that makes your stomach plummet.

The funny thing about time is that you feel you do not have it until something bad happens. Then, all of your time focuses on the very thing you were avoiding.

As much as possible, we need to slow things down. It is possible to slow life down to speed up the areas in which you want to progress.

Sometimes many things are on fire at once, so this can be difficult to do. We must prioritize our time and energy on the front end so we do not have to do it grudgingly as an afterthought.

Many things can be taken down a notch if we are willing to pause, reflect, and slow down before we act. In other words, as a nod to one of my favorite fables, "be less like a hare, more like a tortoise."

I am a constant on-the-go person. It is who I naturally am. It is how I am wired. So, I need the daily visual reminder to be still. As much as I accomplish in my life, I understand that I need calm to have the strength to break the barriers that exist in education.

My internal power is built when I create time and space for silence. The silence builds the ability for me to reflect on my thoughts, if I am willing to let go and be still.

To reinforce this practice, I placed a tiny stone turtle on my dresser. I see this turtle as I enter my bedroom every night. It is the first thing I see before I settle down to my night routine. This is a highly intentional choice for me.

As simple and silly as it may sound, this mini turtle is my regular cue to take it easy. As much as I want to use my influence to solve all of the issues at hand quickly, I know that is not always best. It is also not possible. There is a time and place for everything. Even us go-getters need to unwind. We need to take intentional moments to rest to be healthy enough, mentally, and physically, to do the important work on the horizon.

Let's trust the flow and be more like the tortoise. Let the pressure calm you.

Wisdom often grows at a slow pace over time. Take a deep breath and know that you are on this trying path for a reason.

As much as I would like to press the fast forward button at a 5× speed when the world around me gets tough, I understand that it is not a way to live.

I am reminding myself in times of stress that my continuous belief and dedication always matters more than my speediness. Be one with the current, be at ease in your shell, and keep going.

▶ YOUR INTEREST, YOUR INFLUENCE

We previously discussed the purpose of creating a personal vision. As a leader, we must be aware of our values and interests. It is also pivotal to find ways to align our values and interests with the needs of those we serve. As we know from experience, having a mission is vital, but successful leaders can transform their passions and beliefs to what their students need most.

Let's jump right into it. Your interests can often be the baseline of your influence. What are you genuinely interested in?

Are you:

- Passionate about supporting the whole child while leading staff to do this vital work?
- Driven by lifting others and helping them reach their goals?
- Motivated in making learning spaces more equitable for students?

There are millions of avenues you could be interested in. You could also be interested in many areas. Whatever your fascinations are, name them proudly and find ways to integrate them into your school setting. I have seen, through experience, that your interests can show your unique path to influence.

Would you rather: Learn from someone passionate and invested in what they do? Or from someone who shows by their actions that they are not invested in their work?

> **Hunger brings confidence to yourself and others. The more interested you are, the more invested you will become. Never underestimate the power of your interests.**

Anyone I know would rather collaborate with someone who is fanatical about what they do.

Interest can come at any time in one's life. There is no set trajectory or timeline.

Most, if not all, of my interests have been established through unexpected experiences over time. When I began my school leadership journey over four years ago, I did not realize how my previous experiences would shape my interests today. Time and the life lessons within those years can be the best blessing in learning more about who we are.

My greatest goal as a leader then and today is to make an enormous impact on education that will make schools better and better for kids. Yet how we do this depends on a myriad of factors. One of my greatest interests in education, which did not necessarily exist years ago, is building mental health awareness and students' support.

I have faced traumatic life events that led me to see how crucial mental health support is as a person and professional. My social worker saved my life in many ways. If it was not for my mental health advocate and her continuous support, I know for a fact I would not be writing this book on confidence today. The truth is, I did not have real confidence before beginning counseling. Taking the first step of bravery in gaining counseling support led to continued years of counseling that continue to help me break through the hurt of my previous experiences while breaking free to the life I deserve.

I have a heart and personal testimony for mental health support.

This helps me see and support the families, staff, and students around me that are navigating unimaginable loss. I feel compelled to support in any way possible.

I acknowledge my privilege in how I am able to pay for my counseling supports, while many will not gain these resources due to a lack of finances and outside supports. This is heartbreaking for me to witness and acknowledge. I do not just want to see this occur and be a bystander. I want to do something about this change in the educational space.

Schools are faced with a lack of mental health support for both the students and families during seasons of crisis and through mental health concerns. The COVID-19 pandemic has spotlighted and increased the level of emotional supports that is needed. This new reality is continually forcing us to see how we need to do more from a social and emotional lens for students.

Through my experiences over time, my interest and advocacy for mental health continue to grow. I want to build levels of supports and plans for students, families, schools, and communities. I believe that our boots-on-the-ground efforts in these areas will continue to transform lives, and that brings me more joy than I can put into words.

In December of 2021, I will be completing my Educational Doctorate Degree in School Leadership. Soon after, I will be going back to school to gain my master's degree in social work. I long to be a Licensed Social Worker. Without a shadow of a doubt, this level of training will help me be an even better leader that can shift the way school systems operate to best support students.

Interests are born through time and through putting yourself out there. I would have never known at 17 years old what I now know today. No matter how hard, my experiences have helped me find the person and leader I am as I am writing this book.

I challenge you to use the experiences that you have to build a life of influence that only you can. Your capabilities, your culture, and your life background are beautifully unique to you.

> **Your uniqueness is your influence.**

Please never stop growing, evolving, or leading in our distinctive way. Be you, all the while, staying true to you.

▶ MIND, HEART, & TEAM

Our influence is always shown in our leadership, one way or another.

As Hao and Yazdanifard share in their research journal, "How Effective Leadership Facilitate Change in Organizations through Improvement and Innovation" (2015), "leadership is a kind of power where one person has the ability to influence or change the values, beliefs, behavior, and attitudes of another person."

> ❝The challenging but honest reality is that leaders can make people feel uneasy when shifting the school vision differently. Change is hard and can make us all uncomfortable. Even new practices and mentalities that are best for us are still difficult to accept.❞

Changing one's behaviors and attitudes can be one of the most difficult tasks one can ever take on. Leaders approach this duty each day.

I am naturally someone who works late at night and prefers to go to bed later. Therefore, my early morning alarm clock notification never ceases to annoy me. I know that I need to get up early in the morning to be on top of my tasks for the day. But it still makes me perturbed when I hear the bells sound off bright and early.

The same analogy can be said for shifting behaviors in those we serve as well. We often know the changes we need to make, but it does not make it easier to implement them. Moving a school forward to a progressive course will not always sit well with all stakeholders due to pre-established habits that were previously built over time. We have to remind ourselves and others that learning never ends. Therefore, change will always be occurring. Every single job in every single job sector continually needs reform. On that same token, gaining continuous knowledge keeps our skills in tune with our students' evolving needs.

Hao and Yazdanifard (2015) also share that having influence means that you point your staff in a clear direction. Leaders who do this have strategies, are continually tracking progress, and aim to achieve targets set. On that same lens, to influence effectively, you will inspire others to discover new ways to learn, grow, and collaborate with others.

As we shift the needle of our culture, we will get pushed back. We must stay strong to our vision and use our influence where it matters most to push through any barrier that may approach us.

> **INFLUENCE & IMPLEMENT**
>
> I believe that when we are doing leadership right, our influence shows up in three main ways:
>
> - In the mind of others: New or increased processes, ideas, systems
> - In the heart of others: Growth in care, service, and love for others
> - In our team: Increased vision, collaboration, success, and creativity

The barriers should not stop us. Instead, obstacles help us rethink our strategy and to better align our purpose.

We will not necessarily see these changes occur in big levels all at once. Trust is built over time when our stakeholders see that the direction that we are pointing them, although never easy, is a worthwhile path to take because it is what our students need. We will always have hurdles and areas of growth within our school. No school or leader is insusceptible to this.

As we build faith in one another through our school culture, we will see that influence was the starting point and the continued thread throughout, but that the real influence continues through those around us. Leaders understand that when you create a culture of influence, the best dialogue comes from the students and staff, not from you.

As trust builds, even those who disagree with us will learn that we are coming from a good place.

> **"**We may not always agree, but we need to agree that we are here for kids.**"**

This leverage point of influence is where school pride, partnerships, and knowledge are born. When students and staff members share their minds, hearts, and the love of our team, we cannot wish for anything more extraordinary. This is a goal we can all aspire to.

▶ LEADER LIGHTBULB MOMENT

You may have the direction in which you hope to go. As a leader, you can think of yourself as the compass. But your people are the magnetic force that will navigate you to that direction, or to another, based on your ability to steer.

The best part of leadership is seeing your vision come alive, yet it is even better when it comes to fruition. That feeling is one of the reasons why I keep coming back to leadership, day after day. I love to see progress in the environment around me; it makes me giddy.

When I was a teacher, I lived for the lightbulb moments of students. We all do. We love those moments that you can see a student light up as you watch them work through a difficult task or become more proficient in a skill you have been coaching them through. As a school leader, I live for those feelings with staff, students, and our culture.

When I see a shift in the school culture that did not exist before, I feel like a teacher all over again. I get reminded of why I wake up early each day to do what I do. I see those as God moments that continue to push me in my purpose.

A recent leader lightbulb moment was spontaneously hearing from a couple of parents in my school community. They shared that they feel a positive energy shift at our school. Teachers and students seem happy and have that extra pep in their step. As a result, they shared how inspired they are by my leadership and my heart for kids.

These messages hit me at my core.

Building this environment is exactly what I have been aiming to create, yet it can be hard to have the outside perspective when you are in the weeds.

I know that we will continue to have work to do, yet I needed to hear this.

I was reminded of how our influence can be a human launching pad of new energy and feelings for all those we come into contact with.

Our influence:

- Always matters
- Is more significant than I can put into words
- Has no bounds
- Cannot be manufactured or copied
- Is unique to each of us

Nonetheless, do not let your influence scare you. Instead, allow your leadership to give you the confidence to steer your school to the unknown. Naysayers will try to deviate you from your vision. If you know something in your heart to be true, never believe what they may say.

Believe these truths in your heart of hearts:

- Your vision is not too big or unreachable
- You can do whatever you want to do; do not let old norms corrupt your beliefs
- Just because there may not be a leader who looks, acts, or sounds like you does not mean you are not worthy. You are worthy just for being you

> "As you look inside yourself, know that how you show up in your school will be different than how I lead, or how someone you look up to will lead. Your school's needs are different from mine, impacting how we lead and to what capacity we share our strengths."

> "Your age does not qualify you as a leader. Your willingness to evolve does."

Growth is possible and probable with leaders who have their hearts in the right place and have goals that seem irrational to the outside world. Follow your oddness. Trust your interests. See where they are leading you. Your influence will be what gives you the confidence you need to make it all happen.

▶ GROWING CONFIDENCE

I hope you understand that you have a wealth of influence and nothing or nobody can change that. You have students and people all around you who look up to you. You are someone's role model. You are the inspiration for many.

Nurture your confidence in the way you would for your child; water it because it will not water itself. Remind yourself, especially in tough times, that your influence is unlike anything this world has seen and will ever see. Every experience has made you more resilient and ready for this moment.

Many leaders can make a difference within their school, but they do not fully understand

> "If you don't have the confidence to lead and persevere, even in the unknown situations that come before you, who will? No one is going to step out from their hiding place and save the day for you. Only you can do that."

their power. Leadership is more than having a nameplate that says who you are and what you do. Instead, leadership begins with a person who understands their impact in every interaction they have, every decision they make, and with every step they take in their building.

I started to gain confidence in myself when I realized that not only was I competent to lead but that I was born for it. My eccentricity, boldness, and unique life path did not make me less than anyone else. Instead, it made me the leader that my students needed. I do not want students to see ordinary when they see me because that is not who I am.

I hope that my students and staff can feel empowered enough to do the same through being true to oneself. After all, influence is being comfortable enough to push through the discomfort and promote what you are driven to see.

▶ 3 KEY TAKEAWAYS

- Everyone has influence, whether they are aware of the magnitude of the influence or not. Influence does not ask you if you want it. Influence is a state of being and doing.
- Your personal interests that shift and transform over time will often show your influence effect. The sphere of influence is where you will have authority and inspiration; nothing is more valuable than your irreplaceable life experiences.
- Your will face obstacles as you continue to walk with your purposefulness. They may appear as different beliefs or as naysayers. Do not allow the barriers to alter your vision.

> ❝Be the compass.❞

References

Farson, R., & Keyes, R. (2002). The failure-tolerant leader. *Harvard Business Review, 80*(8), 64–71. https://hbr.org/2002/08/the-failure-tolerant-leader

Hao, M., & Yazdanifard, R., (2015). How effective leadership can facilitate change in organizations through improvement and innovation. *Global Journal of Management and Business Research: Administration and Management, 15*(9), 1–7.

McLain, S. (2018). *The true value of customer experiences* [PDF]. London, UK: Deloitte Development, LLC. https://www2.deloitte.com/content/dam/Deloitte/us/Documents/process-and-operations/us-cons-the-true-value-of-customer-experiences.pdf

Trust Your Gut

Key 3

> **BEFORE YOU START READING**
>
> Within this chapter, you will unpack:
>
> - How to hear and act upon your intuition
> - What it means to be a people pleaser and how to productively move past this mindset
> - Intuitive cognition and how to make the most of it in your leadership practice
> - How to pair analysis with intuitive decision-making to make the best choices for your students and school
> - Unconscious biases you may have stored in your brain and how to release them
> - The difference between self-esteem and self-confidence

I use the phrase "trust your gut." You may call it something else: a hunch, instinct, intuition, or a God feeling. No matter what you name it, the theory is the same. I believe there is such a thing as having a keen and unexplainable knowledge that defies all understanding. You do not know how you know, but you just do.

This intuition can come unannounced and often happens subconsciously.

Your gut feelings are located somewhere between your heart and mind, waiting to guide you and only you.

> **"**Your unique gut feelings are given to you alone; therefore, you have a considerable responsibility to trust and listen.**"**

We often hear this advice—Trust your gut feeling!

Yet, trusting your gut is easier said than done, right? Throughout this chapter, we will unpack this idea of trusting your gut while also giving you research and actionable strategies to make this idea more of your everyday practice.

Following your intuition can be tricky. When a gut feeling strikes, I know what I need to do next and feel called to do so. My vision can somehow get lost in translation between what I know I need to do and then doing it. Can you relate?

Let's be real here; many things can and will get in the way. Sometimes, there are so many blockades behind us, and ahead of us, it feels like we are racing on an obstacle course. When I think of the most significant barriers in my leadership practice, here are the most significant points that come to mind:

- Disapproval from others
- Trying to make people happy
- My inner critic
- Having too much on my plate
- Decision fatigue

The list of barriers can go on and on.

Take time to determine where you are now as a leader. Always keep in mind that reflection is the first step in gaining a grander sense of cognizance.

CONFIDENT SCHOOL LEADERS

As you reflect from reading above:

- What are the three major hurdles in your voyage as a leader? Can you name them?
- Of the three hurdles, which is the most difficult barrier that you are facing? Why?
- How are you currently attempting to overcome these barriers? What is still getting in the way?

▶ PEOPLE PLEASING

As a principal, I find that I am often worried about what others will think of me. I know I will stand up for what I believe in. It is who I am, and it is in my blood. But, after I make the decision, even when it is the right one if someone is unhappy with me due to my decision, I tend to doubt myself.

With confidence, I wish I could say that I do not worry about what people think of me. Yet, that would be far from the truth. As much as it can be a downfall for me emotionally to land into these spirals of thoughts, I also know that I do this because I am an empathetic and human-centered person who leads with compassion. I am an over-reflector. Our greatest strengths can often give us residual areas of growth that stick with us our entire lives.

As a child, I was the oldest sibling in my family. This set me up to be a natural leader and caregiver. I would babysit my brothers at a young age and the neighborhood kiddos during weekly Bible studies. I have always been in tune with the feelings of others. This goes way back for me. My family often shares stories of my days as a toddler; if I saw a baby crying, I would cry and then said with tears in my eyes, "baby crying!"

I sense the emotions of those around me and want to do something about it. I do this to a fault. Sometimes my gut feeling can get intertwined with the feelings of others. I then have to stop myself from swaying away from my intuition.

There is nothing wrong with wanting to make others happy. Yet, if you allow others' opinions to drown out your inner voice consistently, it is time to reassess your needs and actions. We have our instincts for a reason; it knows what your head has not quite figured out yet.

> **❝**We were not called to rely on the instincts of others. We are called to follow our instincts.**❞**

I used to tell myself that I was not a people pleaser. Boy, was I fooling myself. It took me years to realize how much time I spend every day thinking about others and going out of my way for those I serve and love. I do this to the degree that it can take away time, energy, and resources from myself on a very regular basis.

Are you a people pleaser?

▶ YOU MAY BE A PEOPLE PLEASER IF YOU:

- Struggle with sharing your opinion when it is needed most
- Say "yes" when you actually mean "no"
- Pretend you agree with others, even if you do not
- Feel uncomfortable if someone has a different belief than you
- Are easily convinced by the views of others
- Need oodles of reassurance
- Worry about what others may think about you
- Want to make everyone happy
- Struggle with boundaries

> **"** Rather than allowing doubts, distractions, and the voices of others to take up critical rental space in your brain, ensure that you are allowing only thoughtful and respectful feedback to guide you forward. **"**

If you think you may be a people pleaser, do not feel guilty. It is a sign you care deeply for people. Instead, find a way to pivot your mentality from this point forward.

If others' thoughts or opinions come from a bad place and the person does not show care, respect, or love toward you regularly, it is time to separate yourself from the feedback rather than to internalize it. Know when to accept feedback and when to let it go.

As a leader, we are continually gaining feedback from countless individuals: staff members, families, small advocacy groups, and our community. We were not created as humans to take in and process this daily. Therefore, we must place boundaries on these circumstances and lean closer to our instincts.

▶ AN OVERFLOWING PROFESSION

As educational leaders, our plates are not only filled with responsibilities. They are always overflowing with new roles and adventures. This is the nature of leadership.

As funny as it may sound, being a leader can feel like being at a buffet. Overflowing.

As I kid, I thought buffets were the best thing ever. Every food ever created is all in one place and ready to eat! Plus, you can have seconds for the same price. What a deal, I thought!

You can stack your favorites: Cheddar macaroni and cheese, fried shrimp, crispy chicken tenders, hot pizza, buttery rolls, and a dinner salad with ranch—all on one singular plate. People get so excited that they do not want to wait and pack their dishes high. No shame here. I am guilty of this as well.

But have you ever seen someone's food begin to fall on the floor while they are still walking around the buffet? I have. Their food becomes hard to balance, they move too fast, and the food begins to collapse on the floor.

As a leader, this scenario above sounds familiar. We stack our plates tall and do not account for any external variable events to occur. There are countless people to serve and numerous things to do. At times, it can feel like all of the pieces are falling apart right in front of your eyes.

As the long-standing reality TV show Big Brother famously says, "expected the unexpected." I feel this phrase on a spiritual level as a leader. Whether it is contact tracing daily during COVID-19 or problem-solving through a random water break in your school, you have to be pliable and have a thick skin. We are always preparing for the unforeseen. Meanwhile, we are also doing all we can to build relationships and attempt to live in the moment.

As we live in an overflowing profession, we have to do more to let our intuition guide us. If we are frequently in a busy state, we will find it harder and harder to hear our intuition.

Let those beliefs abound naturally and freely from your heart.

As the late Albert Einstein shared, "The intuitive mind is a sacred gift, and the rational mind is a faithful servant. We have created a society that honors the servant and has forgotten the gift."

Find your silence. Stop the chatter. Remember your gift.

> ❝We cannot fill ourselves us by working even harder, making people happy, and earning the false praise of those around us. Instead, overflow with your vision, values, and your belief in students.❞

▶ WHAT IS INTUITIVE COGNITION, YOU SAY?

Research shows that leaders, like CEOs, are inundated with data and decisions. Data and statistics are often demonstrated as reasons to move forward with one choice or another. But what is often not talked about is how and when they follow their gut feeling, or, in other words, their intuition.

Research often names intuition as intuitive cognition. By definition, intuitive cognition is making a decision based on unconsciously recognizing a situational pattern (Patterson & Eggelston, 2017). Intuitive cognition allows one to compare their current reality to past experiences or noticings to find patterns and signs. This is also known as implicit knowledge, which is one's procedural memory. Procedural memory allows you to remember how to do something, even if you have not done it for years. Examples of procedural memory include driving a car, switching a lightbulb, playing the piano, and typing on a computer keyboard.

> **"**The publication also shared how fire-fighters and neonatal nurses used their intuitive cognition to perform their work. Within the research, all parties had significant training in their field of study yet still relied on their intuition to make pivotal decisions 80 percent of the time.**"**

In comparison, analytical cognition is conscious, purposeful, and takes up space in your working memory to execute (Patterson & Eggelston, 2017). This analytical knowledge is also known as explicit knowledge, which is one's declarative memory. Declarative memory is the conscious recollection of experiences, events, processes, and information. In other words, declarative memory takes up brain space.

(Patterson & Eggleston, 2017)

With this said, many times, our brains are unable to determine the best analytical move. We have not experienced yet what we are being asked to do, we do not know the best next step, or we do not have the time it takes to make an analytical decision. This is when our intuition comes in to save the day.

▶ INTUITIVE DECISION-MAKING

As a school leader, when I see this research, I think of all of the times that I relied on my intuitive decision-making skills without even realizing it. In reflection, I find that I utilize my intuitive cognition multiple times a day. The most prominent memories I have of using this skill were during crises or in a significant need.

Intuition will be there to support you, whether you have had years of experience in leadership or whether you are getting your feet wet. My intuition has helped me in many ways, including investigating student discipline cases, supporting students subjected to abuse at home, and creating new school systems to keep students and staff safe in COVID-19 and beyond.

When each of those above situations was presented to me, I had previously never experienced anything like it. Leaders are used to preparing, but even we cannot prepare for every variable. As we know, moments of crisis do not announce themselves before they show up, as lovely as that would be.

Besides,

I will never forget one particular event that occurred an evening I was leaving work. It was getting late, and throughout that day and night, our school was used as a polling place. I stayed late to wrap some things up after school. As it was getting a bit dark, I finally decided that it was time to pack my bags for the day.

> No educational training level can prepare you for everything that you will see and need to know as an educator. Yet, there is something about our God-given intuition and how it tells us what we need to do when the time comes.

As I exited my school and walked closer to my car in the lot, I saw a visibly distraught woman walking around the parking lot, seemingly out of sorts. A police officer was also at our polling place. Around the same time, he also came outside to see what was going on.

In all situations, I do what I can to help. This was nothing different.

Even though I had no idea what was going on, I walked up to the woman and asked her if she was okay. She said she was not okay. She was crying, pacing around the parking lot, and smelt like alcohol. She talked about being a failure and wanting to take her own life. My heart was automatically breaking for this woman. I did not know who she was or what her past looked like, but all I knew was that I could help.

I prayed about it at the moment and felt called and compelled to step in and help her further. I felt this peace and security that this is what I needed to do. I asked the woman if I could take her to the hospital to get the support she deserved and needed. She was adamantly against my idea at first. I stepped back, gave her space, and let her know I was there for her.

The woman continued to pace and cry. It was clear she was processing everything that was going on in her life. It seemed like she was carrying a heavy burden. I sensed that she felt weak and alone.

After several more minutes, she shared she did want to go with me. She wanted help.

The police officer gave me his number in case I needed help, and later on he sent a police officer to meet me at the hospital to support me.

I drove her to a nearby hospital around 10 minutes away. During the drive, she kept apologizing for ruining my night. She shared she had kids at home. She shared she was embarrassed to be found like this.

I reassured her that she had nothing to apologize about and that I was here to help.

Once we arrived at the hospital, I parked and walked with the woman inside. I chatted with the front desk concierge, a nurse, and signed some paperwork. At that time, the police officer came to the hospital to make sure we got there okay. The officer found the woman's information and quickly went to her house to inform her family of what occurred.

In the meantime, I stayed with the woman until she was admitted to the hospital. The whole time, I felt this feeling that I was doing the right thing. I was grateful that I was in the right place at the right time to support her.

One week later at a school event, a former student ran up and gave me a huge hug. To my disbelief, she shared with me that her Mom was the woman I helped the other day. She shared a little bit about what her Mom was going through. She thanked me for caring about her Mom and helping her get to the hospital.

This experience, to me, was a reminder of how strong our intuition can be. I had no idea about the context of the situation before I jumped in, but I knew I needed to do something. I just had a feeling. Little did I know that I would be supporting a former student's mother who was going through the unimaginable.

It is not every day that I would drive a stranger to a hospital since safety is paramount. But, in this case, I felt that it was my calling.

If we rely on our feelings without any intuition, we can often be disappointed.

To add to this, we will find endless benefits of our intuition if we pair them with past analytical decision-making to showcase the bigger picture and fuller thought process as a whole. In other words, if we add our gut feelings to our past wisdom, the sky is the limit.

> "Our intuitive thoughts often feel like emotions. We have to distinguish between our feelings and opinions and our intuition. Unlike intuition, our feelings can sometimes misguide us."

This mix of analysis and intuitive decision-making helps individuals reach peak performance and success, as shared in a research study for first responders (Akinci & Sadler-Smith, 2019).

The journal article thoughtfully titled "If Something Doesn't Look Right, Go Find Out Why" (Akinci & Sadler-Smith, 2019), teaches first responders, such as police officers, a methodology called "Perceiving-Knowing-Enacting-Closing." According to the research, "Perceiving-Knowing-Enacting-Closing" is a framework that captures the complex role that intuition, in combination with analysis, plays in first-response decisions. This framework helps police officers and others perceive what they believe is happening, process it, and check it with the facts and evidence for even better results.

Through additional research by Dr. Jay Liebowitz, Distinguished Chair of Applied Business and Finance at Harrisburg University of Science and Technology, and with colleagues from around the world, the team found that intuition is critical when making executive decisions, even in a business and data-friendly setting (Nolen, 2018).

These research pieces help us draw further conclusions on the importance of intuition in all settings and work environments. There is always a time, place, and purpose for trusting that hunch you have.

Can you think of specific situations where you utilized both your procedural and analytical memory to best support others or a problem? What learnings and takeaways do you have from experience?

> **INFLUENCE & IMPLEMENT**
>
> If you are unsure of how to use your intuitive cognition, here are some ideas based on research:
>
> - To become one with your intuition, seek vital feedback on your intuitive judgments (Sadler-Smith & Shefly, 2004). When you have a gut feeling about something, if it is not an urgent situation that needs to be handled, ask a trusted person to debrief and challenge your initial perspective.
> - As an individual reflection, you can share opposing views from yours and point flaws and blind spots in your intuition (Sadler-Smith & Shefly, 2004). Both approaches help you to see the situation from a different perspective while refining your abilities. With that said, you will continue to gain the confidence needed to trust your intuition and to know when to follow it, and when it may just be your emotions catching up to you.

As you can see, there is great value in growing in the gift of trusting that feeling in your stomach.

▶ CHECK YOURSELF BEFORE YOU WRECK YOURSELF

> ❝With the hustle and bustle of leading a building filled with staff and students, it can become too easy to make decisions out of pure necessity and urgency rather than making decisions grown in purpose. ❞

Leaders who lead well are intentional with all they do, they trust their gut, and always make decisions based on their mission and vision.

See what I said there?

Well-intentioned leaders always make decisions based on their positive set of beliefs. To add to this, leaders who make an impact also make the best decisions to impact students positively. It is a trifecta of sorts, as you can see below:

Intuitive Cognition + Personal Vision + Best Decisions for Students = Instinctual Educational Leadership

With that said, we as leaders are not always right. If left to our own devices, we can make more mistakes and errors than what we feel comfortable even admitting.

Therefore, as shared earlier in this chapter, leaders must seek the feedback of others, especially from those who may challenge you but care, love, and respect you and come from a place of good intention.

Why is this crucial?

Most of the time, when I lead with my heart and intuition, I can come to the right conclusion. But my outcome is always better when I tie others in throughout the process.

> **"** You must check your unconscious biases to trust your gut on a more authentic level. **"**

Other people help me see what I do not see.

Someone else may have a gut feeling in a blind spot that I am unable to see.

We pair our intuitions together, and we can call that collective intuitive cognition, as I am naming it. If we utilize this in conjunction with a strong belief in our school's future, we will become an unstoppable force.

This does not mean that we allow others to be decisive for us, so we do not have to be. Instead, it means that we are uniting our unique gut feelings with someone else, relying on their instincts, and who may have additional knowledge to share. Find others with a deep and genuine soul like yours, and you will be an unstoppable team.

Sounds pretty cool, right?

But all the while we have to be aware of what stops us from moving forward in our school vision and mission.

Do you genuinely reflect on what gets in your way?

What stops you from moving forward in your school vision and mission?

It is possible that what is getting in your way is a barrier mentioned at the beginning of this chapter, or perhaps it is entirely different. Either way, we need to know our blind spots. If you have the best intuition and work ethic this world has ever seen but fail to execute, how are your students and staff better due to your presence? Let's be real here; following your gut requires a heck of a lot of courage and even more confidence in one's self.

We need to check ourselves before we wreck ourselves.

Are you tuning into your energy and gut feelings? Or are you so busy that you cannot even see the trees through all of the weeds?

When we can begin to trust our gut and lead in a way that we are passionate, confident, and proud about from a visceral level, we start to step into our calling of leadership.

▶ HOW DO I GAIN THE CONFIDENCE TO DO THIS?

I must help you understand that your intuition is not your inner critic. For example, if your inner voice is critical and demeans and judges you, that is definitely your critic talking, not a gut feeling.

Your intuition will give you the wisdom you need, and your inner critic will stop you from trying to put it to action. There is a difference. Yet, there are ways to gain confidence in your decision-making through your intuition.

To support in gaining skills and awareness in this area, Nolen (2018) states in her article "New Research Says CEOs Should Follow Their Intuition" that we can see how in tune our intuitions are if we "get a sense for our batting average." It is helpful to see the outcomes of each intuition and to analyze it further. For example: What were the results of trusting our gut? Were you pleasantly surprised, or were there blind spots?

Every experience that we have is a chance to learn more about yourself while improving your forte. I believe we are always growing and always evolving.

You can also test your gut feelings' validity by presenting counterarguments against your intuitions (Nolen, 2018). You can ask yourself the questions below when challenging your hunches. The questions will either validate your intuition as is or help you to use your analytical brain, paired with your intuition, to help you gain even more confidence:

- Does your intuition make sense? How would you describe it in words?
- Does your intuition feel clear and purposeful to you? The best instincts are ones you know, without a shadow of a doubt, you are called to act upon.
- What are the potential holes or missing information? Dig deep to find the facts, events, and details.
- Is there someone that you trust that you can run your intuition by? Have they also had similar hunches?

Through time and intentional practice, you will come to find how your intuition looks and feels for you. This practice will help you gain the confidence you need to set your intuition apart from your emotions and your inner critic. More importantly, as your gut feelings become more and more clear to you, they will continue to resonate with you more profoundly.

This will help you lead your school, your students, your staff, and your community in the manner you were born to lead.

▶ BREAKING UNCONSCIOUS BIASES

As the reader of this book, you must know the reason I have become passionate about the concept of trusting and developing confidence in your gut feelings. I know the importance of this skill from experience and the aftermath that can happen when you do not trust those hunches.

There have been a handful of times in my life where I felt compelled to go after something. In many instances, this intuition has suited me well. For example, I chased after my calling of being a School Principal, even in the face of adversity. I remember hearing the opinions of others and how those negative biases deeply affected me. For example, views were shared such as:

- Male principals seem to be more followed and liked than female principals.
- You need to teach for a specific number of years before being a leader.
- Or my favorite, spending time and money on your Doctorate in Educational Leadership would be a waste.

I believe that very few things in life should be cookie-cutter—originality and differentiation matters. Having an open mind is critical in education, leadership, and life.

I strongly disagree with the idea that females cannot be successful leaders, that young leaders do not have a place in leadership, and that gaining any degree is a waste of money. Students are watching us. If we feel that younger adults cannot lead, this will carry over through a lack of student leadership at our schools. All belong; every individual should be valued, differences and all.

> Building inclusion and equity for all within our school is one of our most significant responsibilities as school leaders.

Let us celebrate the experiences of all rather than only the number of years under someone's belt. As leaders, we will need to work together to break the mold of the unconscious biases.

Trust your gut!

I would not be writing this book today to build confidence in school leadership if I allowed others' opinions to tear me down. I am proud of my younger self for breaking through barriers and believing enough in myself and my intuitions to make my dreams happen.

▶ WHEN YOUR PERCEIVED INTUITION FAILS YOU

I will be brutally honest here. My intuition had not served me well when I ignored it and pushed it aside. There have been several times in my life when I had a gut feeling, but I permitted myself to talk myself out of it. With hindsight being 20/20, I was later left with regret when I did not follow that instinct.

> My best advice is to spend less time guilt-tripping yourself and more time planning your next steps.

This is life. We make mistakes. We are human. We learn. We move on.

I am a self-proclaimed recovering perfectionist. I know how it feels to do the very opposite of what I am recommending; I will always keep it real with you. I can get into my spirals of shame and blame. I will give myself credit because I have greatly improved in this area and know it will be a lifelong goal.

According to the therapist Dr. Spelman (2021), if we make mistakes, the feeling of blame can remind us that we need to do better and give us more accountability. Yet, the blame should not be coming from a place of accusation or ridicule to ourselves or others. We also cannot live in the space of guilt.

If blame is a constant feeling you have, this may be due to a lack of self-esteem.

As we continue to discuss self-confidence, it is essential to note that there is a difference between self-esteem and self-confidence. Some of the attributing characteristics of both terms can be used interchangeably. But, overlap is not always there.

For example, Burton (2015), psychiatrist and philosopher, shares this relationship's complexity. Self-esteem is our "emotional appraisal of our worth." It is the foundation of how we feel about ourselves and interact with everyone around us. Those who have healthy self-esteem do not need outside items to boost their self-esteem. Instead, they invest in themselves and those around them and focus on resiliency over their failures.

On the other hand, self-confidence is "to trust in your ability or aptitude to engage successfully, or at least adequately with the world." A self-confident person loves to push themselves, try new opportunities, and take on challenging endeavors. All the while, a confident individual is so in tune with themselves. A confident leader will own up to their mistakes (Burton, 2015).

It is possible to have high self-confidence but a low self-esteem. It is also possible that you could have high self-esteem and confidence in some areas, but not in other areas of your life. The relationship between self-esteem and confidence is fluid, different for all, and continually changing. Awareness of who we are and how we feel is an essential part of being a leader.

The goal is not to be perfect or to have confidence in every area. Instead, our goal should be to mindfully grow while aiming to reach our personal best. What that looks like will be different for us all.

Learn from this process and evolve as a leader. Think of everything as an experience meant to put you one step closer to your continued purpose.

▶ COACHING MOMENTS: FOR YOURSELF AND THOSE YOU SERVE

One of the best things we can do as a school leader is to coach others to trust their gut. We should build people up around us like it is our job because it is!

As I mentioned in the intro of this book, during a recent Whole-Child conference I presented at for my school district, I asked the question, "What is one of the biggest barriers getting in your way right now?"

Nearly 100 people attended my session, and many of the chat's comments revolved around a common theme of lack of confidence and doubt in oneself. Reading these comments helped to reinforce why this book is necessary for so many.

> ❝When I break down a handful of the many things I do as a leader, one of the top areas that I spend a big chunk of my time is helping others to gain confidence.❞

To illustrate this, while being a school leader, it is critical that you:

- Serve as an instructional coach for teachers
- Hire and train teachers and staff members
- Co-lead and co-create learning and professional development opportunities with your team
- Develop the skills of staff members to prepare them for a variety of roles
- Help your school community to see the importance of our continued evolution as a professional

When you synthesize the roles above, you must be intentional in how you coach up others. Your role as a leader is to develop yourself to be the greatest you can be for others. School leaders today are more than managers of people. You are the influencer of everyone you serve. To be an influencer and help people be their best, you must walk the walk and talk the talk.

Ask yourself the following questions to validate or push where you currently are:

- Do you model what it looks like to be a continued learner? In other words, do you practice what you preach?
- Are you in the know of what the best practices are today?
- Do you find ways to connect with others, inside of your workplace and in the global surroundings?
- Is creating a community of dedicated learners, adults, and students important to you?
- Is dialogue created to continually push your school mission and vision forward to reflect our students today?

Yet, I must say this: Whether you are new to leadership or a seasoned veteran, do not stop being curious or asking questions. There is a reason why the phrase lifelong learner is always said in education. Some people mock the term or find it redundant, but there is a plethora of truth to it. As professionals in the realm of education if we ever decide to stop learning and evolving, we need to be brave enough to exit stage left.

Educators and learners should always learn. That is our role. We should accept and promote nothing less as school leaders.

With that said, coaching moments are all around us to build confidence in others. Seize on those moments and understand that your goal should be to spend as much time developing yourself as you do others. It will never be even, but the goal remains.

How do I know this to be true?

From trusting my gut.

We all know the feeling. Out of the goodness of your heart, you spend most of your time building up others, so you forget about yourself.

On the other hand, if you only focus on growing your knowledge base and you do not feel compelled to build up those around you, you may feel over-confident, while those around you may feel unworthy of your time and efforts.

> As leaders and educators, we need new learning just as much as those we serve to keep our fire alive. If we do not, we can feel depleted or under-confident in ourselves.

I believe that even the most "stuck in their ways" educator craves someone to care about them.

In the next chapter, we will dive even further into methods and strategies to support those around you. Influence is best felt when we can see others growing as a result of our efforts. Healthy confidence can foster when we take the time to develop it!

> We will continue to love while pushing others to be their best for our students.

▶ 3 KEY TAKEAWAYS

- Our intuition, or our intuitive cognition, can be tested and developed. Instinct can be even more beneficial when paired with facts and further understandings. Trust that hunch you have and allow it to be part of your continued practice as a leader.
- The unconscious biases that we have can stop us from stepping into our purpose as a leader. Challenge your perspectives and those around you. Know when to listen to the voices of others and when to shut them out.

> Be the leader you have dreamt of being, not what others want you to be.

- There is a difference between self-esteem and self-confidence. Understand how both concepts show up and how they integrate within your life. You must feel worthy to take risks and to be open to new challenges.

References

Akinci, C., & Sadler-Smith, E. (2019). 'If something doesn't look right, go find out why': How intuitive decision making is accomplished in police first-response. *European Journal of Work and Organizational Psychology, 29*(1), 78–92. doi:10.1080/1359432x.2019.1681402

Burton, N. (2015, October 19). Self-confidence versus self-esteem. Retrieved January 31, 2021, from https://www.psychologytoday.com/us/blog/hide-and-seek/201510/self-confidence-versus-self-esteem

Nolen, M. C. (2018, December 18). New research says CEOs should follow their Intuition. Retrieved January 25, 2021, from https://chiefexecutive.net/new-research-says-ceos-should-follow-their-intuition/

Patterson, R. E., & Eggleston, R. G. (2017). Intuitive cognition. *Journal of Cognitive Engineering and Decision Making, 11*(1), 5–22. doi:10.1177/1555343416686476

Sadler-Smith, E., & Shefy, E. (2004). The intuitive executive: understanding and applying 'gut feel' in decision-making. *Academy of Management Perspectives, 18*(4), 76–91. doi:10.5465/ame.2004.15268692

Spelman, B., (2018, January 07). The weaponisation of shame, blame and guilt. Retrieved January 25, 2021, from https://theprivatetherapyclinic.co.uk/shame-blame-and-guilt/

Key 4 High Expectations, High Support

> **BEFORE YOU START READING**
>
> Within this chapter, you will unpack:
>
> - The power of feedback: How to model it and when to accept it from others
> - How to properly address underperforming leadership
> - How to navigate tough conversations with others, while reframing the way you view these discussions
> - What it means to show care, while having boundaries simultaneously
> - The importance of keeping communication open and fluid with colleagues, mentees, and beyond

As a school leader, "high expectations and high support" is not only something that I often say when making decisions for our school, but it is also something I live by. I take this expression very seriously in my own life as well. I genuinely believe that you cannot have high expectations without high support. In my mind, the two go together.

When schools only focus on high expectations while lacking supports for students or staff members, the culture can feel hierarchical. Yet, if the school community has a plethora of supports without boundaries, the culture can feel like a free-for-all.

As confident school leaders, we must find the right balance of high expectations and high supports. You want your school to feel neither methodical nor disordered. Instead, schools should have a clear sense of purpose and direction while focusing on professional collaboration and collegiality for all.

Throughout this chapter, we will explore how vital high expectations and high support are for yourself and those you serve.

▶ RESPONSE TO FEEDBACK

To me, leadership is about empowering all.

What does leadership represent and mean to you? How would others describe the type of leader you are?

These questions matter. Often, how we define it is not necessarily through our words but how we show it in our actions.

Regardless, we must be able to hear the assessments from ourselves and others while finding a way to serve others better as a result. Some critiques are meant to sting and leave a burn. Some analyses are intended to see you thrive. True leaders know the difference and have high expectations for themselves anyway.

As we discuss feedback, we must note the importance of understanding when to accept others' advice and when to leave it. We need to grow continually, but we cannot evolve if we spend more time listening to others' opinions rather than trusting our instincts to lead.

There is always push and pull of doing what is best yet hearing opposing views. This is the epitome of leadership; there are still ebbs and flows.

> **❝**When comments and opinions are stated with the intention to bring you down, that is not constructive criticism, nor is its feedback. Feedback is something given to someone else, with the best intentions, to help them be even better.**❞**

Yet, let us be real here; most people do not know how to give feedback that others will receive. In other words,

We must train others on how to provide feedback that is rooted in integrity but covered in grace.

As leaders, we are often taught ways to deliver useful feedback, but the same professional development is often not given to those we serve. Rather than waiting for the training

> **CONFIDENT SCHOOL LEADERS**
>
> - Model how to give meaningful feedback through their everyday, informal interactions. Think beyond the formal meetings you may have
> - Can be trusted to be honest, while giving strategies and resources for others to grow
> - Help build instructional practices through input and coaching that is always student-centered
> - Think of how to build grassroots efforts within their school community, by empowering teacher leaders with the training and skills to coach up others

to come, let us coach others through our modeling and individual conversations.

▶ SET A REALISTIC, HIGH BAR FOR YOURSELF

First and foremost, it must be said that you have to have high expectations for yourself to make any meaningful changes occur in your school. School leaders cannot just have high expectations for those around them. They must also have them for themselves as well.

This does not mean that setting high bars for yourself equals perfection. Trust me, I have made mistakes and have fallen short of my abilities as a leader. When this happens, and mistakes are made, you get yourself back up, wipe away the grime, and show up anyways. Just because you are a leader, that does not mean you are somehow immune to being human. We are all humans, doing the best we can, learning as we go, so we will repeatedly:

- Fail
- Embarrass ourselves
- Make countless mistakes
- Wish we could go back for a re-do

In the education world, there is often this need to be perfect. We feel shame over our mistakes. Therefore, we like to put on an invisible mask. A mask that falsely shows that we have it all together. The pressure we put on ourselves is immense.

For the record, setting the bar high for yourself does not mean expecting faultlessness; these are two very different things.

I struggle with this balance myself. Due to past traumas in my life, I have always expected so much out of myself. I believed I needed to be everything for everybody. This belief system is a lot to take on.

Through support, I have grown drastically in this area and will continue to do so. Meeting with my counselor has taught me more than I can express. One of the most meaningful takeaways I have had from therapy is that my unrealistic expectations are hurting me more than helping me. I learned that I designed these standards to make myself better, but the relentless inner need to always be on my A-game is exhausting. Through being real with myself and through therapy, I have continued to learn about who I am.

Maybe you can relate to my invisible struggles.

We, as leaders, are whole people. We are more than a school leader. We have families, personal lives, people we love, and a past, present, and future. We are not one-dimensional. Many of the schemas we need to break away from are created from other places in our lives. This is why it is crucial to becoming one with who you are. Be proud of you: the messiness and all. Going through what we have grown through is one of the best things we can do for ourselves as human beings and as school leaders.

Remember this: As educators, we are in the business of learning. What does learning revolve around? Knowledge is often built from our efforts and mistakes. You cannot learn anything without making some. Permit yourself to be human, let your guard down a bit, and learn through doing. After all, it is the only way you will get the most out of your voyage as a leader.

▶ UNDERPERFORMING LEADERSHIP

As an educator, I have seen educators and school leaders who were not performing at their best level. When I mention underperforming, I am not referring to someone going through a rough patch of their career or navigating a hard-hitting season of life. I am referring to a continual pattern of an individual putting the minimal effort forward and being disengaged in their work day after day, year after year.

Sometimes this lack of leadership is due to:

- A lack of skill
- A lack of will
- Your heart not being there (*going into school leadership for the wrong reasons*)
- Personal reasons
- School politics

We have all witnessed leaders who lack skill and will. When willpower is not present, the school culture and student performance will always suffer. Schools who succeed do so in large part to their leader setting the tone. Leaders create the foundation necessary for schools to be all they can be for students. As Sun and Leithwood (2012) share in their work "Transformational School Leadership Effects on Student Achievement," "Leaders are almost always responsible for improving the technical core of their organizations' work. In the case of school leaders, there is an unrelenting demand to focus on improving all students' achievement, making contemporary school leaders' attention to instructional quality the highest priority for their work."

It may be possible that leaders who initially began school leadership did not quite understand the many roles you would take on: relationship builder, budget master, instructional leader, professional development creator, school discipline expert, facility leader, family and community connector, and beyond. Yet, suppose we want to continue as school leaders. In that case, we need to take the initiative to develop ourselves personally, dig deeper into our strengths while building upon the responsibilities that do not come as naturally to us.

Leadership will not always be comfortable for the leader. If it were, that would mean that you were content with the status quo, while most likely not pushing yourself enough. Either option is unwelcome.

If you decide to continue your path as a school leader, you must understand that it is a lifelong journey. Stay committed. There is no glass ceiling to break. Yet, the passion within you must be strong and continually lit from within.

Honestly, it is hard for those you serve around you to be inspired if you are not engaged in your role. As Bolman and

> When the school leader is checked-out, others will follow suit. That is the harsh reality.

Deal (2008) stated in their work, *Reframing Organizations*, leaders who recognize how to evoke spirit and soul can form a more unified and effective organization. Yet, it is hard to bring that spirit to your school if you lack it yourself.

It is important to note that we all get in a funk. The funk can be due to a variety of reasons. Rather than feeling guilty for feeling less than ourselves, we must be self-aware. We need to take care of ourselves and notice these signs to help shift the pattern, rather than allowing disconnection to become our new baseline.

If school politics is getting in your way or your current school is not the best fit for you, it is time to reevaluate your next steps. You influence your life. Are there other roles or school districts that better align with who you are? Would a new opportunity help you to bring out the joy in you again?

> Confidence is not thinking you have all the answers. Confidence is the belief that you can move through any barrier with hope and resilience. Be self-aware and continually move forward as you pivot and adjust.

It takes courage to put yourself out there, and you have that bravery within you. Never feel stuck. You have one life. Think of every role as an experience that will get you closer to where you want to be. Do what is best for you!

School leadership takes continued dedication. If we take the pledge to be a school leader, we need to check with ourselves if our heart is still in it each year. Sometimes, all you need is a boost of confidence.

▶ WHAT MESSAGE ARE YOU SENDING?

Whether we are trying or not, we are always sending messages. Messages are sent in many ways, through our subconscious behaviors and our intentional actions. Teachers can tell if you value their ideas, care about instructional practices, and if you value risk-taking by merely watching your routine as a leader.

For example, if you have high expectations for collaboration yet do not seek input, you may lose others' faith. If you ask for teachers to be creative and pioneer new practices, you do not model this philosophy; your words will quickly evaporate.

As I continue to lead through COVID-19, I have let my staff know that even though we are building the plane as we are flying it, if their intentions are to best support our students, I will always support their efforts. I want my school community to take risks and to put themselves out there. It all is a trickle-down effect: If I model the behaviors I want to see; hopefully, it will trickle down to staff members, which will inevitably trickle down to our students.

At my school, we have regular grade-level collaboration meetings with our administrative team scheduled during teachers' plan periods; we book the whole day to this work and individually meet with each team. The work is essential, so we carve out the time to support our teachers instructionally while supporting student growth. I am an instructional leader to my core, after all.

Due to staff shortages resulting from COVID-19, I have had to think outside the box on how to support our teachers. Especially during one particular collaborative day. On this day, we had countless unfilled staff absences, which means that teachers were absent, and we all put our minds in overdrive to problem-solve and cover classrooms. Therefore, I knew that day was not the day to have the typical meeting format.

Instead, my instructional coach and I quickly developed a plan B. We recorded our meeting virtually while presenting the important learning and prompting reflection questions and action steps that teachers would complete later. We were able to flip the learning on the fly without compromising the work. This allowed teachers to watch the video while diving into their learning, reflections, and next moves.

When staffing obstacles approached me that day, I had an important decision: Should I cancel the meetings, reschedule, or forge a new path?

It is often easier to cancel the meeting and to call it a day. Sometimes we do need the time and energy to decompress and to gain our bearings.

Yet, always, always, remember this: Leaders still have high expectations for themselves before even asking anything of others.

To reflect, how do you show up at your school, district, and community? If you were an outside observer, how would they describe the impact you have already had on your school and district?

Remember that you cannot just have high expectations for yourself. You must show love and grace to your soul, too. The question is not: Are you a lousy leader? The prompt to ask yourself is, how do you show up well, and how can you break barriers to be even better?

▶ SHOWING CARE AND BOUNDARIES

One of the most complex ideas surrounding leadership is navigating and balancing supporting others while also holding high standards. It can be challenging; I am not going to sugarcoat it.

To be honest, I received zero training on this topic before jumping into the principalship. Luckily, I did learn a lot through experience as a former teacher leader and district leader. I have continuously made efforts to pick others' brains around me to navigate different situations to gain a more excellent skill set. Why wait until you are a school leader to learn the ins and outs when we have school leaders all around us?

It came naturally to me to serve others and know when to jump in and support, but it took much more practice to navigate challenging conversations. I wanted to avoid these conversations like the plague itself.

Each time I had to have a conversation such as this with someone, I used to take on their mistake as I did it myself, rather than understanding that the error is separate from the individual and me. Coaching others becomes much more of a more effortless flow when you accept this element.

Sharing what is going well is easy for most. Who doesn't love to share the good while celebrating those around them? It uplifts your soul and makes others, and yourself, feel on top of the world!

Yet, things get a little tricky when you know that you need to have a more difficult conversation in your heart of hearts. Usually, you know when there is that constant gnawing feeling. Those chats are not always sunshine and roses, even if you pre-plan every agenda item. Even with skill and experience, conversations like these are not why I get out of bed in the morning. Regardless, they are still essential.

One of my friends and colleagues, Dr. Jason Theodorakos, shared a nugget of wisdom that has since stuck with me. Theo, as I call him, said, "Tough conversations are not tough after all. Just think of them as simple conversations."

It may sound simple, yet the idea is loaded with empowerment.

We often load actions with strong words, such as "tough or courageous conversations," to help others approach the dialogue. Still, I often wonder if this language and mindset may have the opposite effect.

For example, if I frame my brain into thinking, "This conversion is going to be tough or difficult to have," I may have an experience that lives up to my expectation.

Instead, if I reframe my thinking to set an overarching goal instead of using the conversation to clarify, ask questions, support, and share expectations, it seems much less heavy of a chat. This is an area I continue to grow in and will continue to gain confidence in overtime. I still use the terminology, tough conversations myself, yet how I perceive it continues to evolve.

Another way of thinking of it is calling people in rather than calling them out. If we call people in while being honest, truthful, caring, and transparent, we lead from high support and high expectation, which is the gold standard. Leadership is always a balance of care and boundaries.

In each situation, I always ask myself, how can I stay committed to this individual while also empowering them?

Empowerment is the best thing you can do for all you serve: students and staff.

Students also need high expectations and high support to thrive.

> "If we only call people out while leaving out ways to support them, we lead from a place of frustration and authority. Yet, if we help others while leaving out our honest thoughts and specific strategies, we walk into the coddling zone. Support is always different than coddling."

> "Why keep knowledge for yourself when you can spread it to others?"

▶ TOUGH LOVE

My assistant principal, and dear friend, Amanda Buhr, described my approach in two words better than I ever could myself. She shared that I lead with tough love. It is simple yet accurate. Sometimes the phrase tough love can be misconstrued or misinterpreted. In all honesty, this approach also is received well more from men than from women. Yet, my vision of tough love has less to do with being tough but more to do with being honest, genuine, and caring—all three qualities thoughtfully wrapped up together. I have also tagged this phrase—gracious accountability. It's a dichotomy that is essential: loving the people you serve while holding expectations that tie with your school's mission and values.

This is my philosophy when interacting with all people. I believe we must be honest, but we do so with love and empathy. If we do not speak from an authentic place, our influence will lose its luster. In my opinion, any feedback should come from this place.

Although I am leading through my first official year as a head principal, I have placed myself in countless previous leadership experiences that prepared me for this moment. Between my experience, intuition, and passion, I feel made for leadership. I hope you feel this in your bones as well. Let us lead from a place of genuine truth and support. Most people would rather hear the truth in a caring way, even if it is hard to hear, instead of being misled with fabrications, to make someone feel better.

Let's permit ourselves to lead with gracious accountability. After all, this approach works.

According to the journal article titled "Hard, Soft, or Tough Love Management: What Promotes Successful Performance in a Cross-Organizational Collaboration?" these beliefs are validated, even in the realm of business and start-ups. Kelman and Hong state (2015) that "Improving performance of teams in start-ups" is "caring about fellow team members' needs" and "making expectations explicit." Kelman and Hong noted that tough love does not necessarily mean showing love, yet showing care in a way that may come across direct is the only way to help someone in the long term.

Long story short, informal accountability helps all members hold one another accountable. This helps to spread the responsibility to all. Informal accountability is beneficial, yet it needs to be paired with gracious accountability from school leaders.

When we reflect upon our approaches as leaders, we must understand that we are the pulse of the building. We must be grounded in our moral purpose to have intentional conversations that will lead to lasting change and effects in our staff and

> **INFLUENCE & IMPLEMENT**
>
> Clearly expressed and purposeful feedback is more effective than informal accountability. Examples of everyday accountability in schools are:
>
> - Creating agendas, norms, and roles for meetings
> - Instructional peer walkthroughs in classrooms
> - Staff-led committees that support the building mission and vision
>
> What are ways that you embed informal accountability into your school structure to help those you serve be the best they can be?

community. We need to spend less time second-guessing ourselves and aligning our actions to our values. Instead, trust your gut and do what needs to be done.

In other words, what are you doing at this moment that will build the future that your school, community, and world needs?

▶ MENTORING THE MENTOR

I believe that current leaders need insight, confidence, and approval to follow their gut from a current leader who is living it. More times than not, we as leaders do not gain the permission to be the leader we need to be.

During this year, I have trained and coached my two brand-new assistant principals as well. We are all navigating our first years in our specific roles; what a journey, primarily through COVID-19. Although this is year one of us being together, we have been working with each other for months leading up to this school year. We have been continually working tirelessly to best prepare and support our community.

One thing that we have continually seen is how teams drive success. It is incredible to do amazing things by yourself, but it is even better to do amazing things with others. Life is not about passing the torch to others, nor is it about providing opportunities for them. Instead, it is about empowering them to be who they were called to be. Along the way, as I lead with honesty and care for them, I am also continually asking for their genuine and open feedback so I can grow upon my practice. Our friendship and camaraderie help us to continue to build collective efficacy together.

As I have coached and worked beside my Assistant Principals, I always tell them that I am not only preparing them to be a great Assistant Principal, but I am also preparing them to lead a school of their own one day. I am thinking ahead. My bigger goal in supporting them, and all staff, is to help them gain the confidence and skills to take on their next adventure, whatever and wherever that may be.

I am passionate about mentoring others since I have seen the impact it has had in my own life. I have had leaders who have cared about building me up not only in my current role but also for the future. These leaders saw my strengths and pulled my potential out from within me. This is such a gift that we can pass on to others—mentoring those around us in hopes that it will make a difference not only in their lives but in the lives of others.

Feedback, coming from the right place, is what all educators and leaders need. We all deserve a mentor who cares enough about us to be both real and encouraging. Balancing both approaches in a way that feels authentic to you is essential. People can spot realness. Sometimes, tough love can be just what we need either to reassure us or to help us forge a new path.

We are a lot like our students. We need someone who will believe in us. Someone who will have high expectations for us while guiding us along the way. Mentors matter.

The importance of mentorship is explained in a nursing research article titled "Strengthening Mentorship for Leadership Development" (Jeans, 2006). Jeans shares that mentorship is integral to leadership, especially among diverse professional groups. A mentor relationship is always professional but can build into a friendship that is important for all employees. When mentoring is done best, a mentor and mentee are matched with needs, learnings, and professional goals. During mentorship experiences, both the mentor and the mentee grow. Mentors help the mentee to success that may not have been possible without them.

In addition to enhancing success in one's career, "mentorship has been associated with higher job satisfaction, higher income, increased confidence, self-esteem, promotion, and advancement (Jeans, 2006)."

It is important to note that mentorship does not always have to be a formal process. It can be an informal bond that spontaneously occurs with another person. How the mentorship begins is not as important as what you gain from the process.

One of the most influential mentors I have ever had is Dr. Megan Stryjewski. She is our district's Assistant Superintendent of Teaching and Learning. Dr. Megan, as we call her, is knowledgeable, approachable, real, and understanding. Even amidst her chaotic schedule, she takes the time to meet with me biweekly to check-in, see how I am doing, and give me essential feedback. She asks what she can do to support me and what type of feedback I most need each time I meet with her.

I have appreciated Dr. Megan's investment in me. It makes all the difference to have someone that you can bounce ideas off, who will give you wisdom, and who will not make you feel like you are losing your mind while doing so.

> When we keep the communication open and fluid, all feedback and suggestions become more natural, rather than an awkward or singular event to be wary of. When someone cares enough about you to invest in you, it makes all feedback feel welcome and inviting.

As leaders, you become an unofficial mentor to many.

All along the way, do not forget to invest energy and time for your personal development, too. Mentors need mentorship as well.

▶ STOP WALKING ON YOUR TIPTOES

Marion C. Blakely, the President and CEO of Aerospace Industries Association, once said this, "You can't leave a footprint that lasts if you are constantly walking on your tiptoes." This way of thinking completely resonates with me. We often have the foresight to know our next steps, yet we are walking on our tiptoes, too afraid to do what we know we need to do.

Sometimes leadership can feel like you have a wedge underneath your car tire. You push on the gas, want to accelerate, yet you are stuck. Sometimes we are metaphorically the wedge underneath our own tire—your own worst barrier. Yet, sometimes, our desire to please people can be the wedge. If we want to make a lasting influence on those around us, we need to be honest with ourselves and honest with others.

Honesty can be challenging for the receiver and the giver; yet, most people would rather hear honesty from a place of love than falsities. Just like everything, it takes practice and development in the skill set. Over time, you will build trust with yourself and those around you as people gain the comfort level of working beside a leader who is coming from an authentic place. In a world where everyone is trying to be someone else, it can take people off guard to see a leader who is walking in their purpose.

Your leadership and influence matter.

You are there, not just for those who admire you. You are there to serve all who you interact with.

As leaders, we can ask ourselves: What can I do for others rather than what can they do for me?

Often, the best thing you can do for others is to be disciplined in trueness and goodwill.

You will not be perfect at this, but you can be self-aware along the way. Find the lessons in every experience. Even in those moments where you came across as either too harsh or impressionable.

> **❝** To have high expectations with high support, you must lay the groundwork day after day. It is not always easy to live from this place; it takes radical self-truth and belief on your end. Be vocal about what matters to you. **❞**

Your wisdom and life experiences are just as unique as who you are. We often take for granted just how uncommon we are. Do all you can not to lose sight of yourself.

We are marked to live a life that is different than anyone else. Therefore, your influence will be just as individual as you. No one can make the difference you can. No one can say things the way that you can. Use these experiences to help navigate how you guide others.

When you speak your truth, you can rarely go wrong.

▶ 3 KEY TAKEAWAYS

Confidence is not thinking you have all the answers. Confidence is the belief that you can move through any barrier with hope and resilience. Be self-aware and continually move forward as you pivot and adjust.

Tough love or gracious accountability is a gift you can give to others and yourself. Gracious accountability takes commitment to someone else and cares for who they evolve to be. Whether you are a kid or an adult, everyone deserves a mentor and someone who is just as dedicated to their growth as they are.

Clearly expressed feedback is highly influential in supporting and coaching others. High expectations paired with high support takes intentional thought and practice. Find the formula of both that speaks and works for you. Speak from an authentic place while following your compass as a leader.

References

Bolman, L. G., & Deal, T. E. (2008). *Reframing organizations*. San Francisco, CA: Jossey-Bass.

Jeans, M. (2006). Strengthening mentorship for leadership development. *Nursing Leadership, 19*(2), 28–30. doi:10.12927/cjnl.2006.18170

Kelman, S., & Hong, S. (2015). "Hard," "Soft," or "TOUGH Love" Management: What promotes successful performance in a cross-organizational collaboration? *International Public Management Journal, 19*(2), 141–170. doi:10.1080/10967494.2015.1114546

Sun, J. & Leithwood, K. (2012). Transformational school leadership effects on student achievement. *Leadership and Policy in Schools, 11*(4), 418–451.

Be the Calm in the Storm

▶ INTRODUCTION

> **BEFORE YOU START READING**
>
> Within this chapter, you will unpack:
>
> - How confident school leaders embrace change and become one with it
> - Fear-mongering and how to shift limiting beliefs
> - The differences between stress and burnout
> - How to push through principal burnout while creating lasting boundaries for yourself
> - How to stay grounded in your purpose as an educational leader

Let me start with a question for you: Does your best work happen when you are rushed or when you are mindful? Easy answer, right? Sometimes, we can succeed when we are hurried. Either out of luck or due to our body adjusting to repeated crisis mode. We are more resilient than we often realize. But, if we frequently succeed with intention, time after time, we need to be more mindful in what we do.

We can choose to be in crisis mode, or we can choose to be more intentional. We know this, yet it is easier said than done. We do and need to continue to do the crucial workaround simple practices that take disciplined commitment.

What do I mean here?

I cannot say it enough, but we must take the time to sit down and listen to our inner voice. There is constant noise around us. We always hear the expectations and demands of others and honestly fear. Fear is a normal feeling, and it often approaches us in leadership.

> **“**Confidence is not the absence of fear. Confidence is feeling the fear, looking it straight in the eyes, and moving forward anyway. Confidence in your leadership is standing up for what you believe in and not backing down. Sometimes our movement ahead may be a small step, while other times, it may be a bolder dive into the unfamiliar.**”**

The message that I often share with my staff is that change is the constant in life and education. That is a hard pill to swallow for most. Especially during this current season of COVID-19; change is happening every hour, every day, every week now. One minute, we have updated mask-wearing and quarantine procedures, and the next thing you know, all practices change.

I love to have a sense of control in my life, yet this experience has reminded me that the only thing we have control over is our reaction to the circumstances around us.

Trust me; there are plenty of moments when change is incredibly uncomfortable for me as a leader. Especially when it comes to soaking in others' reactions as they face change, change can be hard on some folks. As a result, I have become the queen of bouncing the negative responses from others and turning them into gold.

> **“**Transformation in schools begins with building rapport while simultaneously shifting ingrained beliefs and developing system-wide approaches that did not previously exist before you.**”**

I have faced these experiences first-hand as I continually work to transform schools.

This work is necessary yet far from easy.

It is a tough spot to be in when your school needs help right now. You cannot idly sit by. You must move! When moving forth with the change, pushback will always be a side effect.

It is often comfier and cozier to settle in with what we already know. With what we know comes expected outcomes, behaviors, and familiarity. Our brains are wired to find structures and patterns in everything.

▶ FENCES OF FAMILIARITY

Familiarity can be such an incredible thing. It can bring a sense of home, love, safety. As I think of this, I am reminded of one of the greatest loves of my life, my nephew, Westin. Wes is obsessed with his stuffed animal black cat named Bella. He named it after his real-life black cat, Bella. Adorable, right? Wes carries Bella, the stuffed animal, around with him everywhere! Then, each night, Wes brings Bella right back home to bed. Bella gives Wes feelings of safety and security.

Change often brings the opposite feelings of safety and sanctuary. Change and transformation can bring big emotions such as fear, a sense of danger, and even doom and gloom. Also, employees experiencing change worry that their organization will no longer be the place they loved or related to. They can think: Maybe my workplace is outgrowing me and the long-standing practices.

An organizational change and a rebrand of the mission, vision, and core values can threaten those who find their identity with how the organization used to be.

Even when change is necessary and practices need to be developed for the better, change leaves an unsettling feeling for those experiencing it. People wonder: Will I have the skill set required to thrive in this new environment? What if I do not want to change and like how it used to be?

George Bernard Shaw, a political activist and playwright who lived to be 94-years-old, discussed change beautifully with this quote: "Progress is impossible without change, and those who cannot change their minds cannot change anything."

We must be able to change our minds and see change as a possibility of hope. As leaders, we must be the ones to cultivate it in others. This is not a microwaved and fast-paced process, but, instead, more like a rotisserie-style process. It takes time, will, and patience.

Familiarity can be the giant fence that blocks us as a leader. Yet, we can use this to our advantage and the advantage of others.

> **"Turn the familiarity into change and that change into gold!"**

Venus, Stam, and Knippenberg of *Harvard Business Review* (2018) conducted research in two case studies that showed how leaders could gain success during change. What they found is "in overcoming resistance to change and building support for change, leaders need to communicate an appealing vision of change in combination with a vision of continuity. Unless they can ensure people that what defines the organization's identity—"what makes us who we are"—will be preserved despite the changes, leaders may have to brace themselves for a wave of resistance."

In translation, leaders must be proud of the change, and the rationale for the change, while also reminding those they serve of what is continuing and the explanation and context for why change is necessary. Even through change, we can still honor those around us while pushing our school forward. Our kids need our model of resilience.

> **"** Leaders who are calm in the storm accept change first and foremost. You cannot be a confident yet humbled leader if you do not become one with ever-changing circumstances. **"**

It does not mean it will always be sunshine, rainbows, and kittens, but the work will always, always be worth it.

▶ BEWARE OF FEAR-MONGERING

Leaders who are here for a positive influence do not arouse fear. Instead, leaders model that change is not something to run away from. Calm leaders, who push mindsets and embrace discomfort, are those who find success.

What does it look like to foster an environment of fear?

- A lack of mission and vision: Those you serve do not know what you believe and where you are going
- Pressing blame and shame onto others: Central office, students, colleagues, parents
- Pessimism: Giving into negative mindsets and promoting said beliefs
- Leading from a reactive brain, rather than seeing all things in a solutions-focused lens
- Letting storms run you rather than owning each storm

You most likely have seen leaders or educators who have embodied some or all of the bullet points above. I know I have. It can be incredibly disheartening to witness.

Sadly though, fear-mongering is all around us.

By definition, fear-mongers take the action of deliberately arousing public fear or alarm about a particular issue. Sometimes fear-mongers are discreet, and sometimes they are loud and pronounced. We all have seen fear-mongers do their thing first-hand. Let's cut to the chase; they are good at what they do. They can gaslight positivity while investing their time poking holes in hopeful change. All in all, fear seekers are part of the problem in front of you, rather than being a team member and partner to find the resolution.

> ❝Schools must move past living in a state of fear and moving into what is doing what is best for kids, whatever that takes, and whatever that means for your school and your students.❞

As a leader who has been called to transform schools, I find fear-mongering the #1 occurrence that gets in the way of moving schools forward.

The fears we do not face as leaders become the limiting beliefs we live by. Whether it is your fears or the fears of others, the fears will run away from you when you face them head on. Yet, if you run away from fear, it will always find you. Leaders instead lead with a robust belief system, facts to guide their decisions and consequently do the hard things.

▶ THE THING ABOUT STORMS

Leaders as a whole have hit a whole new level of exhaustion lately, and rightfully so. It seems like we are facing storm after storm recently: Whether it is political, racial injustice, or COVID-based.

We often wish the storm would pass but forget that we add fuel to the fire or create our storm. It can become all too easy to have an automatic negative response to certain situations. We give excuses, complain, and blame those around us for what is occurring around us. Accountability is crucial, but unnecessary blame is different. When we name faults, we are allowing scapegoats of excuses to enter our spaces. When we do this, we give the green light for negativity to continue.

What do you stand for?

We need to rethink our actions, reestablish who we are, who we want to be, and what we want our school to evolve. We can allow the negativity around us to lead the school culture or unapologetically put an end to it.

▶ THE STORM INSIDE YOU

Have you ever felt like the storm was raging inside of you? Not an external storm, but an internal war that is silently eating at you? A feeling of job burnout or leadership withdrawal is a telltale sign of this.

You may wonder: What is leadership withdrawal, anyways? I coined the term leadership withdrawal to describe a phenomenon I have seen many times. When a leader is overwhelmed between demands placed on them, decisions they need to make, and perceptions others have on them, leadership withdrawal occurs.

Leadership withdrawal can cause someone to have decision fatigue. Instead of showing the leadership skills they possess, they showcase a lack of desire and initiative for solving the issues at hand. This can result in a lack of confidence in one's skills and a lack of trust from your employees.

Whether you have been in school leadership for countless years or are starting your first year in administration, you are not immune to this. Even if you have not reached the point of real burnout, you have probably had moments where you sensed yourself feeling dysregulated. During those moments, all we want is the weekend at home to recuperate.

There is a difference here between stress and burnout. Therefore, before we continue, let's not mix the phrases interchangeably or overgeneralize either term. Although lines are very blurry here, the main difference between burnout and stress is that burnout can occur from accumulating many stressors or events over time. I have added the differences in table form for easy reference (Dike, 2018).

As you can see from the Table 5.1, there are similarities and differences between the two. We all experience stress, yet burnout is a magnified and constant feeling of emotional helplessness. It is also important to note that burnout can be affected in multiple areas: physical, cognitive, emotional, or a combination of all three elements.

Table 5.1 Stress vs. Burnout

Stress	Burnout
Overengagement	Disengagement
Reactive or overactive emotions	Blunted or distant emotions
Sense of urgency and hyperactivity	Sense of helplessness
Lost or diminished energy	Motivation is lost or diminished
Leads to anxiety	Leads to feeling depressed
Physical tolling	Emotional tolling

We all have seen alarming statistics and news articles of school leaders who stop working within schools due to high burnout levels. You may know a school leader who left the profession due to these feelings or is on the verge of doing so. A 2010 study written and created through the Association for Supervision and Curriculum Development, Simon Fraser University, and George Mason University found correlations between the causes of leader burnout and what can be done to combat it (Stephenson, & Bauer, 2010). This study gained information from 113 Louisiana School Principals who served a variety of different demographic communities. According to this piece,

> "Principal isolation is a predictor for new Principal burnout."

Below are the items and definitions of terms that can cause Principal isolation (Stephenson, & Bauer, 2010):

- Role Ambiguity: Uncertain feelings about which behaviors are and are not appropriate
- Role Conflict: Occurs when there are incompatible demands placed upon a person relating to their job or position
- Role Overload: Exists when an individual fulfills multiple roles simultaneously and lacks the resources to perform them. It can evolve from both excessive time demands and unreasonable psychological demands

> **CONFIDENT SCHOOL LEADERS**
>
> - Ask for help and ask clarifying questions when they need to
> - Communicate concerns they are experiencing within their roles, along with potential solutions to their supervisors to problem-solve. Remember—If you are facing something difficult, it is likely that another school leader is, too.
> - Find community with other school leaders where you can gain emotional support and ideas from
> - Pay it forward and coach up others who need guidance

- Social Support: Having friends, peers, or family to turn to in times of crisis to give you a broader focus and positive self-image
- Coaching: Process that aims to improve performance in the present. It helps others learn how to maximize their potential.

Additional highlights from the study (Stephenson, & Bauer, 2010):

- Role ambiguity and role overload are statistically significant predictors of isolation
- Social support serves as the most significant predictor of principal isolation
- Role conflict fails to emerge as a significant predictor of isolation

As a school leader who is relatively fresh in the field myself, I can connect my own experiences to this research's findings. Especially as we continue to be more and more digital while having the majority of our meetings virtual, isolation becomes a familiar feeling. I crave connection and sound advice from others.

As a school leader, I rarely become stressed because incompatible demands are placed upon me. Instead, I feel stressed or dysregulated when I am unsure what is expected of me, when too much is on my plate, or when I am unsure who to turn to for pressing situations. The hardest part of being a leader is when you feel alone. I bet you as a leader can agree with many of these same notions.

During my three years as an assistant principal, my training included a Summer New Administrator training. Unfortunately, I received only one meeting with my mentor throughout the course of my assistant principalship. I lacked mentorship, guidance, and support. When I wanted to become a better me, I had to seek out these opportunities and initiate contact with others I did not know. It takes courage and vulnerability to do this, but it can and should be done.

As I mentioned earlier, we cannot tell the storm to stop. We need to calm ourselves from the inside. There are some things we may not have control over: district-provided training, district mentorship, how often you can meet your mentor, and situations occurring outside of your control. But what you do influence is how you initiate other forms of networking and support, whether provided to you or not.

> **"** Whenever I feel isolated, alone, or in my feelings, I find that talking to a trusted leader, whether in my surrounding area or not, helps me gain a fresh perspective and different ideas. Often all I need is someone to listen to my thoughts and experiences. We all need a sounding board and someone to affirm our experiences. **"**

We all want to hear that there is validity to our experience.

▶ THE PRESSURES WE FACE

There are immense pressures we face as school leaders. Unless you are or have been a school leader, you may not understand it. If you have not led during COVID-19, you would also not understand the new realities.

Being a school leader takes a special type of person who has a wild commitment to their practice.

We are often tasked to lead under various circumstances: financial and resource constraints, a vast political landscape, lack of district leadership past or present, and community dynamics outside of our control. We also sometimes walk into a role where we are asked to turn around a school that was previously struggling. It can often feel like we are thrown into situations without training, support, or the backing of others. These are the pressures we face!

Through all of these circumstances, we still must lead.

No matter what comes before us, we should and will always make an influence and impact on others. We will find our center

> **"**Through all of the outside chaos, never lose sight of what you are there for. Our kids! There is not one student we cannot reach, or not one student who cannot achieve. Student achievement should be seen and measured in many factors: social, emotional, cognitive, and physical. Student achievement is not just academic growth.**"**

of calm and keep moving mountains for our students. It is what we do!

I see student achievement through a variety of everyday interactions with my students. The other day, one of my dedicated educators and paraprofessionals shared a heartwarming student achievement story: A brilliant student with autism consistently walks the same path in our building each and every day. He craves structure and routine and previously would be disinterested to walk through certain hallways that were unfamiliar to him. One day recently, out of the blue, he took the paraprofessional's hand, walked to a new hallway, and found a new path, all on his own accord. She came to me, so proud of our student, and could barely share the entire story without crying! This is student achievement.

> **"**Although it is tougher now than ever to be an educator, it is even tougher to be a kid today. Remember why you are here.**"**

Through all the pressures, see the joy and tenacity in every experience and through every triumph. These moments of hope are all around us. Let's cling to them and promote them throughout our school community.

▶ WHO IS YOUR SHOULDER TO LEAN ON?

We can drive ourselves mad looking at a myriad of ways to solve problems yet feeling stuck at what to do next. I assure you that someone out there has the advice you need. You just have to ask. It takes time and extra effort on your part, but it is worth it if it helps you become a more confident and competent school leader. As school leaders, we can also build informal collective networks if they do not already exist. I have done this very thing, and it has made all the difference. It does not have to be a formal suit and tie affair. All you need is a small and caring group of leaders who will listen, share, and love one another through it all.

Just as our students and teachers need someone to love them up, we need the same.

Who is your shoulder to lean on? Can you envision their smiling faces in your head as you read this?

As a head principal, I am now involved in a leadership cohort experience and have a mentor who I meet with regularly. Praise the Lord! This is truly the first time in my career that I have had this.

No matter what your circumstances are, advocate for yourself! Can you sign up for a leadership mentorship experience, or can you join in on a leadership professional development opportunity in your region? Can you attend a professional learning conference and connect with someone new?

When there is no opportunity near you, find a new path, and if the course does not exist, create one yourself. As leaders, we continually see glaring needs that others do not see. These are signs of gifts that we have to contribute to our school system to make it an even better place. Stressors are often outside of our control, but we have the authority to shift our perspective and to find calm. Look for peace by listening to what your soul needs. Then, make it happen! We need to stop trying to calm the storm and calm ourselves first. Everything you need is within you waiting to be released: inner love, inner love, and inner peace.

▶ BOUNDARIES ARE NOT A BAD WORD

One of the differences between the leaders who are on autopilot and the ones that are in charge of their path is one word: boundaries.

Anytime you see a leader who bites off more than they can chew, I can guarantee you that this individual struggles with boundaries. A lack of limits can look like this:

- Saying yes to everything
- Struggling with giving tasks and projects to others while preferring to do it all him-/herself
- Staying at work until the late hours of the night
- Taking on all of the emotions of others as their own
- Responding within a nanosecond of someone sending them an email, text, or call

How do I know all of this?

Real talk: I know this because I used to actively do all of these things on a very regular basis. I am a recovering " yes" leader.

I would do it all: stay the latest in the evenings, answer every email the soonest, and take everything off everyone's plate. As I look back and reflect, it felt like I was in constant competition with myself to help the most people in the least amount of time.

Do you know what eventually happened to me? I felt terrible. Awful. It was the worst I have ever felt in my life emotionally, physically, and cognitively. I felt like a shell of a person once I would get home. I barely had any energy to come home and take a shower, let alone work out, eat healthily, or take care of myself.

I was sleeping terribly, overeating, feeling self-conscious, reeling with anxiety, and caring about everyone else except the feelings inside of me. Self-neglect, my friends, is not okay.

My work and my job became my entire existence and my whole identity. My work became my escape from reality. I was navigating traumatic experiences, so my work was my getaway. Yet, the release turned into an obsession.

Do I love what I do? Absolutely! Do I feel called to be a leader? Yes, I feel it in my bones. But should my entire persona, or yours, be wrapped up in a job and a job alone? Nope. I hope I have struck a real and honest chord here with you because it needs to be said.

> **Anytime you feel yourself becoming overly obsessed with work, it is a signal for you to pause and remember that you are a whole person who needs to be cared for as much as your students and staff. Take a break. Let it go. Walk away from it all for a bit.**

We talk about self-care like a summer vacation or taking an hour off looking at emails throughout your entire evening. Self-care should demand much more out of you than this. We must give ourselves more as leaders and raise the bar even higher.

Life is but a blink, and stress is a mind, body, and soul killer. We forget this when it comes to ourselves. We want others to create those boundaries and create new policies to make our jobs more mentally healthy. But, we disregard the fact that we are accountable for this work as well. We are parts of the system. We can do better to create boundaries for ourselves and others as well.

My counselor often says to me: "No one will say to you, Kara: Are you taking enough care of yourself? I know you have been going through a lot as a new Principal. Are you taking enough time for yourself? You should!"

It is rare that many people will give you this advice, so you can go ahead and stop waiting for it. Instead,

Back to me here: Can I do a better job of not answering emails in the middle of the night? Yep, that's on me. Can I do a better job of being on vacation when I am on vacation? Do I need to stop responding to work emails and be more present with my family? Or, do I need to stop mentally thinking about work even though I am not there. Yes, those are on me, too. My bad, yet again.

> Be that strong inner voice for you. Love yourself the way you love others. Be the mother in yourself that you need.

But, let me tell you something I am immensely proud of. For the first time, I created a new boundary for myself. If you are reading this and already do this, praise yourself and your skills! But, for me, this was a huge accomplishment: This past summer, I decided to take my earned vacation, set the out-of-office email, and not look at my email for two weeks. Not at all. Not once. Was I tempted to look at my emails or work? All of the time, but I did not look once.

With a new mindset, I was able to better see what was an emergency that needed to be addressed now and what could wait until later. I also gained more assertive discipline in myself; when I felt the urge to work, I learned to say no. I have continually learned and reaffirmed with myself that boundaries are not a bad word. Instead, having limits should be celebrated and continually grown.

As school leaders, we often run around frequently, as our lives depend on it. We treat everything like it is urgent. We run instead of walking forward. Rather than leading mindfully, we approach everything from a crisis mindset. To put it lightly, this is not healthy for students or staff.

Running is necessary sometimes, figuratively and literally. Take yourself out of the equation for a second. Is it essential for a leader to act in this manner at all times? No, no, and no!

Some people may respect your tenacity in the short term to handle things quickly, but for others it will make them nervous. Very few want to see their leader nervously running around. This does not give others confidence in you or a sense of safety and security. Often, our behaviors need to be reflected upon. What we demonstrate as a leader will be followed and emulated, whether we like it or not.

Do you want others to walk forward on purpose while enjoying their life? Or do you want them to be a task machine who has forgotten why they began in education in the first place?

As we walk in our purpose, National Leader and formal Principal Kafele shares a nugget of wisdom: "Burnout will be inevitable if a leader is overwhelmed with work that doesn't contribute to his or her inner purpose. If you find this becoming your reality, reexamine your 'why.' Determine if your work as a leader is corresponding with that purpose. If it isn't, it becomes incumbent on you to determine why not—and make whatever adjustments you need to move toward once again walking in your purpose (Kafele, 2018)."

With this said, are you walking toward your purpose, or have you gotten so far away from it that it is a distant memory? If we forget why we started this role in the first place, we are in trouble. Moreover, the student we serve is in trouble. We need to be thoughtful in why we do what we do and how we get to point A to point B in our work. If we are not careful and mindful, a lack of purpose will ruin us.

How are you continually pivoting as a result of your learning in leadership?

One of the many mantras I have created is, "I will lead rather than be led." This does mean that other people cannot teach me. But, to be a confident leader filled with influence and purpose, I need to lead myself. It is not healthy to allow adverse experiences, thoughts, or outside individuals to call my shots. I know within me what I need to do and how I need to lead. If we are authentic to ourselves, we will not lead in a way that is like anyone else.

It is often an hourly mantra for me, but I am getting more proficient at living it over time. If our goal is to be perfect as a leader, I am afraid we got leadership all wrong. Newsflash: If you want to be perfect in leadership, it will never happen, and it should not happen. We are humans after all with imperfections and vulnerabilities.

Leadership is about serving others with all of our heart and soul as best as we can. This requires us to be 100 percent dedicated to ourselves and our work while finding the calm in what our soul needs. Go after what you need: I promise that it will bring you peace.

▶ NORMALIZE CARING FOR YOU

It is heartbreaking to see school leaders who are continually burned out and running on autopilot. To calm in the storm, it will require you to own the mindset of walking in your purpose so you can give back to your school community.

> **"** Normalize caring for you. Put yourself first in your life. Please stop considering yourself as an afterthought. When you can normalize it caring for yourself, you will inadvertently normalize it for others as well. **"**

What we practice, we show in our daily actions, habits, and subconscious beliefs.

Teachers also need extra love and care, now more than ever. If you ask teachers to take on this work, it will reinforce that the work is impossible if they can see that you are not living it. But, it is not impossible. It is difficult and will take continued discipline, but it is possible.

Besides, it is essential to note that our students will not thrive if we do not lead from this place. If we are not our best selves, but we expect students to be their very best, we are fooling both our students and ourselves.

Through it all, three things have made the most significant impact on my personal development: counseling, leaning into the real me, and connecting with those who love and care about me, and my success has made all the difference. Yet, I almost had to hit rock bottom to see the bright rays of light. I still have rough days and weeks, but they are never rough months or years. Through self-growth, I have continued self-awareness. I wish the same for you.

Reflect: What are two small or big things you can do to normalize caring for yourself? How can you hold yourself accountable in this work? Write this down either digitally or on paper, where it is visible to you every day. Make you the first and next priority in your life.

INFLUENCE & IMPLEMENT

"What does my mind, body, and soul need now?"

Ask yourself this daily in order to give yourself what you most need. Do what feels right to you in any given moment. On some days, it may be extra rest, while on others it may be an energizing walk or a dinner out with your significant other. Do not apologize for saying yes to yourself.

▶ **3 KEY TAKEAWAYS**

- Transformational change will make others feel uncomfortable as they adjust to the school's new mission, vision, and identity. Build continuity in previous practices that are best for students and the school while also confidently walking forward. Lead with purpose and intention. Help others continually see who you are, what the school is capable of being, and how you will get a team. Do not sell yourself short. Be proud of the positive changes!
- Role ambiguity, role conflict, and role overload are three factors that can lead to Principal burnout. Stressors are very different than actual burnout. When we sense ourselves feeling overwhelmed and defeated, we must reach outside of ourselves. Ask for help, do everything you can to change your current circumstances, and find people who can be your shoulder to cry on. We all go through highs and lows, but we need to recognize when we are frail and depleted.
- Insane pressures are upon us as leaders. Although our jobs are tough, it is even tougher to be a student today. Do not lose sight of why you said yes to school leadership and what drove you to this position. Be centered in your purpose. Be the strong yet calm force that your students desperately need.

References

Dike, C. (2018, June 12). Stress vs. Burnout–What's the difference. Retrieved March 01, 2021, from https://blog.doctorondemand.com/stress-vs-burnout-whats-the-difference-429547f5d82a

Kafele, B. K. (2018). Avoiding school leadership burnout. *EL: Educational Leadership*, 55, 22–26.

Stephenson, L. E., & Bauer, S. C. (2010). The role of isolation in predicting new principals' burnout. *International Journal of Education Policy and Leadership*, 5(9). 1–17. doi:10.22230/ijepl.2010v5n9a275

Venus, M., Stam, D., & Knippenberg, D. (2018, October 14). Research: to get people to embrace change, emphasize what will stay the same. Retrieved February 28, 2021, from https://hbr.org/2018/08/research-to-get-people-to-embrace-change-emphasize-what-will-stay-the-same

Stay on Your Path

▶ INTRODUCTION

> **BEFORE YOU START READING**
>
> Within this chapter, you will unpack:
> - Finding the right leadership path for you
> - The importance of sweat equity in your career and continued growth
> - Determining the best fit for you in your next journey of leadership
> - How to combat decision fatigue to feel more focused as a leader
> - Viewing self-reflection as an art form for continued growth
> - Thinking in shorter bursts to make long-term plans more actionable

In March of 2021, my husband, Stephen, and I tied the knot. I went from Principal Welty to Principal Knight, all during our earned Spring Break. If this year is not wild enough, we decided to get a second dog the day after we returned from our honeymoon.

We drove three and a half hours away, to the middle of nowhere, to pick up our baby Basset Hound named Honey.

Now friends and readers, let us fast forward in time to today.

It is a gorgeous Missouri Sunday in April, not a cloud in the sky. Stephen and I wanted to make the most out of this weather, so we took our dogs for a walk. We chose a park with a 4.4-mile loop to help give our first and wild pup, Maple, a chance to exert all of her energy. On the other hand, Basset Hounds are not known for their athleticism, so Honey stops walking at 0.65 miles every time. It is like clockwork.

As a proactive plan, we brought a stroller to push Honey around once she pooped out. Never in my wildest dreams would I have guessed that I would be the girl pushing a dog in a stroller, but, hey, that's me now!

Imagine this: We were two miles in our walk, and Maple was getting wildly distracted by other people and dogs on the trail. At the same time, Honey was literally trying to leap out of the stroller. To say we had our hands full was the understatement of the year. Therefore, we were not paying attention to signs of the different paths that lied ahead of us.

A fork in the road approached us up ahead. The folks in front of us turned right on their bikes, so we did as well, without thinking twice. The further we walked this new path, the more remote the surroundings looked. We had no idea what was going on or where we were. As we looked all around us, we did not know how long the road ahead was and when we would get back. We were by a highway now far away from where we began.

We decided to turn around, and luckily, we did.

At this point, we had already walked five miles, and with our considerable delay, our walk was not even halfway over. So the four-mile walk was turning into a ten-mile expedition. Not to mention, we ran out of water, the dogs were getting antsy, and we were feeling frustrated by the situation.

To add to the stressors, I knew I needed to get home to write this chapter of my book. So the deadline for turning in the first draft of this book was on the horizon after all.

After we made a U-turn on the walk, we became more mindful and figured out where we needed to be. Slowly but surely, we made our way back to our vehicle, safe and sound.

Ironically, hours later, as I sit down to write this chapter, I realized that today's experience, as annoying as it was, was showing me a hidden lesson.

▶ THE WRONG PATH FOR YOU

How far must you go down the right path to realize that it is not the path for you?

I wish there were a hard and fast rule, but the truth is there is not. Only you know the answer to that question. Trust yourself.

But one thing is for sure, no matter where you are now, even if you are down the wrong path for yourself, you can always turn back around.

Today, we were on the wrong path for us, but that does not mean it was the wrong path for the bikers ahead. The bikers were equipped and trained to tread the countless miles ahead of them. We were not.

In leadership, we are each equipped differently so that we can lead differently.

But, too often, we focus only on the destinations we want to reach rather than the slow and tedious learning process. We also can find ourselves wanting the life experiences of others rather than finding peace and purpose to where we are now.

> **❝**The wrong path for one could be the right path for someone else.**❞**

All of the time, I have people share with me that they want a teaching job, a leadership job, or to even write a book. Yet, when I press further on what they have done to reach their goals or ask them questions to hear more about their dreams, I am

---

CONFIDENT SCHOOL LEADERS

Throughout this book, we have discussed being one with your vision and goals. As you gain comfort and confidence in this work, I want you to reflect deeply to ensure that:

1. Your dream is YOUR dream and not someone else's
2. You are following your path because it speaks to you, not because someone else is doing it
3. For any goal you develop you are willing to put in the work required to make it happen

> We all reach times in our life where we feel seasoned, or we need the seasoning; sometimes, we need both at once.

> Your path to leadership is a relentless and ruthless journey to awaken yourself. You will be continually pushed and challenged in every way imaginable: spiritually, emotionally, physically, and cognitively.

surprised by the typical responses. To be honest, I often hear more silence than answers.

I feel compelled to speak to this because throughout my career I have continually seen leaders who need repeated confirmation and affirmation from others to the point of their self-detriment. These leaders seek advice, not to grow, but to survive.

Yet, if you constantly ask for permission from others to lead in the way you need to lead, you are not one with your path. You will never be happy if you live someone else's idea of leadership instead of your own.

Do not fall asleep to reality. Instead, listen to what your experiences are trying to teach you. Allow those lessons to guide you further rather than to freeze you in place.

▶ NO QUICK FIXES

There is no quick fix to gain knowledge, have the degree you have been aiming for, or get to the next level in your career. There is no substitute for patience, hard work, volunteering up a time to learn, and relentless hours of understanding behind the scenes.

Although I started my administration career when I was 29, every year of my teaching career was leading up to being a leader. I was involved in countless pursuits after school and in the evening to better myself. I focused my time learning from others, diving into different leadership roles for my school and district, and I often volunteered my time for free. I even used my personal days at work to shadow other leaders I admired. We only get two a year, so those days are precious! Yet,

> What you value and focus on is what will grow.

Even in college, there was a long period where I worked over part-time hours as I went to school full-time. I sacrificed many college experiences to work at a preschool for students with special needs. As a result, I learned more than I can express while also providing for myself.

Countless hours of work have led me to where I am today, and the same applies to you.

We cannot idolize the end result more than the trials and tribulations that occur along the way. Without the obstacles, you have no destination. It is all a part of the process.

We will each get to our own Point A to Point B, somehow and someway. Sometimes, it takes several other stops to do so. Or sometimes, we may start over and start anew.

This hard work, or sweat equity, that you invest in your abilities as a leader will help you build your way.

What is sweat equity, after all? Sweat equity is a common term in the business world that speaks to the **unpaid labor employees and entrepreneurs** put into a project or work. When you are genuinely passionate about something, you often naturally put the sweat equity into it. In addition, engaging in sweat equity means you want to improve your practice and believe in your success.

As Mark Cuban from "Shark Tank" says, "Sweat equity is the best equity there is." Cuban and the other Sharks never invest in those who do not seem entirely and hopelessly committed to their business's mission. It makes sense, right? Self-made millionaires and billionaires do not want to tag their names with individuals who have not shown they can triumph over adversity and factors beyond their control.

Let's be honest, though: Educators are the real pros of sweat equity. We know what it is like to spend unpaid time doing what we love for a cause greater than us.

It all boils down to what we do with our time.

On my best days, after I get home from work, I am using my sweat equity to write this book and dive into projects to help my school reach new heights. These are goals I set, so I schedule out times on my Google Calendar when I will make it happen. But I still have days where I am not feeling it, too. On those days, I am using my spare time to scroll through social media aimlessly. Using my time like this never makes me feel good afterward.

My challenge for you is to break down how you are using your time. As school leaders, we are exceptional at scheduling our workday on Google Calendar to the minute. But, before and after school, it can be a struggle to be as disciplined. So, as you break down how you are using your time, reflect on the following questions:

- How much time are you spending on your phone, apps, social media, etc.? Are you happy with that time you are spending?
- Are you scheduling personal items that will help you get closer to your goals? Think of experiences such as your goals, working out, any personal passion projects you have wanted to do, or simply building in time to update your resume and look for your dream job.
- Are you building in regular times for rest? Do not wait for the weekend. Instead, give yourself time each day to stop your brain. Whether it is 5 minutes for meditation, a 15-minute stretch, or a 10-minute reading session—DO IT!

> See yourself as an ever-growing person and leader and give yourself time to check in with yourself, your mind, and your body to know what you need and how you can adapt based on how you feel.

There are no quick fixes to finding your path, especially since our path constantly changes since we are always evolving. So instead,

▶ SELF-REFLECTION AS AN ART FORM

As a school leader, are your current goals and actions aiming you to be where you want to be and who you want to be?

My dear friend Cameron Poole (2021) is the epitome of meshing his career with his life goal as a leader. Cameron is one of the rare people you meet and meeting him instantly feels like he is walking in his purpose.

I had the honor of working with Cameron when we were both Assistant Principals and being alongside him in my doctorate cohort as well.

This past year, Cameron transitioned from High School Assistant Principal to Director of Equity in Inclusion.

As a young man, Cameron saw the need for change in education and knew he could actively do something to best support the kids around him. Cameron is passionate about creating school environments where students can be treasured for who they are. So, when the role for a Director of Equity and Inclusion was created in a nearby school district, Cameron went for it!

Cameron has a blog on his school district's website called "The Equity Corner Blog." Cameron invests in his work while being transparent and sharing it with others he serves. For example, in a recent post to his community, Cameron shared (2021):

> I usually end most learning sessions with strategies and questions to ask our students and parents to better understand their experience. Our district professional development on April 30th revolves around forcing us as a district to *self-reflect*, by engaging in the viewing and activities around filmed conversations, with various underrepresented groups within our district population. *Self-reflection* is key. We have to fall in love with the process of *self-reflecting* before we can engage in actual equity work. Otherwise, we are fighting an enemy that we can't recognize or identify.

Cameron's points of prioritizing self-reflection are paramount in every learning and growth process.

> **"**If you are not reflecting, you are not learning.**"**

Furthermore, as Cameron stated, we need to fall in love with the process of self-reflecting. It may not always be a comfortable process, but it is a necessary one. If we truly invest in ourselves and those we serve in a big way, we must ask the right questions. Regular self-reflection with yourself as a leader is also paramount to stay in tune with who you are, where you are going, and if you are on the right track.

Recently, a once in this lifetime opportunity opened up, and a couple of colleagues shared with me that I should go for it. I was honored they thought of me and began truly contemplating if I should go for this new adventure. As I was self-reflecting, I reached out to Cameron to get his perspective. Here are some of the spot-on questions he probed me with:

- What is the benefit over your current job?
- What is your ultimate goal in education?
- Will that move bring you closer to that goal?

As I continued to reflect upon my questions and Cameron's, I realized that although this opportunity was rare and unique, it was not for me. So, I decided not to apply. I knew deep in my heart that I instead wanted to continue to dig deeper and invest in my current work. I felt and feel in my bones that I have more work to do.

Sometimes the new and shiny will approach you, and the best intentions and opinions of others will begin to seep into your brain. These suggestions from others may even begin to alter your decisions without you even realizing it. Yet, ultimately, will your potential move help bring you closer to your goal in education or not?

In addition, when a new opportunity arises, I think it is also essential to ask yourself:

- Does this new opportunity get me revved up?
- Is the timing right?

Leadership is not about reaching someone else's expectations. Instead, leadership is doing what you are passionate about in the timing that feels good to you.

I often see leaders who lead in a way they think they should lead, rather than being true to who they are: actions, endeavors, and priorities. Do what feels right to you and no one else.

Many decisions we contemplate as leaders are difficult ones. I urge you to spend the time necessary to reflect and tune in with yourself. Self-reflection is genuinely an art form we as leaders need to continue to cherish.

▶ INVEST IN YOURSELF

At a coffee shop, I once saw a chalkboard sign that said, "You will be around longer than that expensive handbag. Invest in yourself." I felt that this sign was coming after me!

Earlier in the chapter, I challenged you to dive into how you use your time to use what time you do have more wisely. We can also take this a step further and look at how we are investing in ourselves. Are we doing so with full pizzazz, or are we going through the motions? In other words, do not invest in yourself superficially.

> ❝In all seriousness, we invest in many things as humans, but how often do we invest in ourselves?❞

In the book, *Running with the Mind of Meditation*, Mipham (2012) writes:

> In the modern culture of speed, we seem to not do anything fully. We are half watching television and half using the computer; we are driving while talking on the phone; we have a hard time having even one conversation; when we sit down to eat, we are reading a newspaper and watching television, and even when we watch television, we are flipping through channels. This quality of speed gives life a superficial feeling; we never experience anything fully...When we are running ... we are engaged in one of the most intimate and meaningful acts that might occur during the day.

Although this metaphor was written to describe running, I could not help but make connections to leadership as I was reading this book. For example, how often do we feel that we are half listening to others, half engaging in meetings, and half participating in the task in front of us because our mind is thinking about something else? Or, we believe we are multitasking when in reality we are just distracted on two tasks rather than actively engaging in one.

Unfortunately, society is fast-moving and prizes fast results over detail-oriented and slow-paced work.

Let's be real here, as leaders, all of the following things are often happening at the same time:

- A parent is on hold, waiting to talk to you on the phone
- An Individualized Educational Plan (IEP), meeting is about to start, where your participation is needed
- A student wishes to speak to you to report an incident that happened in class
- Emails are infiltrating your mailbox
- Budget timelines are due and waiting to be approved
- Teacher and staff evaluations need to be typed and submitted
- A staff member needs to talk to you about a personal emergency

With many items pulling for your attention at once, it can be challenging for your brain to settle. This makes it problematic to prioritize and focus on intention. This can cause us to act impulsively, attempt to do multiple things at once, or engage in work avoidance. As mentioned in "Chapter 5", it can be hard to be the calm in the storm when we are constantly bombarded with decisions to make.

Even more specifically, decision fatigue can hit us even further since our decisions are not often straightforward. According to Dr. White (2020) of *Medical News Today*, you are more likely to feel the effects of decision fatigue if you do the following:

- make many decisions throughout the day
- feel significantly affected by the decisions they make
- make very stressful decisions
- make very complex decisions
- make decisions affecting other people in a significant way

Without even hearing your reflections, readers, I know that you are engaging in all of the above items if you are a school leader. Let's be honest! I know how it feels! When you go home, your mind can feel spent. As I continue my journey in leadership, I have done the following to help me prioritize myself:

- Remove distractions when engaging in complex tasks or with sudden deadlines

    On social media, we see leaders who are on their desks on wheels throughout the school day. We often hear messages on social media that leaders cannot lead from their office. I believe that we cannot generalize statements such as this. Although I am a leader with a desk on wheels, I will close my office door to complete complex work. I often get distracted by the sounds around me and need time to focus on an important project or deadline. Do not feel guilt or shame in doing this.
- Know the strengths and roles of each member of your team

    No matter your leadership role, we can put unnecessary pressure to do all things ourselves. I have improved in delegating work to others, while knowing the strengths

and functions of my leadership team. As a result, when a new project or task approaches, based on our strengths, each of us has confidence in who will lead what task. This way of thinking helps to minimize stress while building collective efficacy in each of us.
- Press the snooze button on emails

    Thank you, Google Calendar, for creating the snooze button! If I see emails in my inbox, I feel that I need to respond immediately. I have continually improved in prioritizing the order in which I respond to emails. I love snoozing things for later in the day, so the email is out of sight and out of mind when I am working on an important project or engaging in a meeting that warrants my full attention.
- Take a breather

    I still feel guilty doing this, but I force myself to take a breather on days where I need it. My favorite breather break is walking outside on our student track for two laps. I always have tennis shoes with me at work! So, when I need it, I take that time outside to walk it out and refocus on myself.
- Add to your calendar personal items and projects to stay focused

    To write this book, I devoted my time on the weekends to complete it. I booked the days I would work on it through my Google Calendar and stick to it. Are you more of a paper planner person? Either way, do what works for you and prioritize your goals.
- Reformat how your day looks

    Some days you may feel more self-empowered than others, yet we must still focus on ourselves. It is not selfish to care about your personal development. However, you cannot be the best leader for others if you do not invest in yourself!

▶ THINK IN SHORTER BURSTS

With all of this talk on self-investment, it is also paramount that we discuss how we view goal-setting as a whole. As we just discussed, we have a myriad of items to process as leaders each day. Yet, we still must set goals for our school and ourselves.

Setting long-term goals can overwhelm you and permit you to think in shorter bursts of time instead.

As we know, we cannot predict the future. We are not mind readers. But we can approach our future a bit differently. In the podcast "How I Built This" with Guy Raz, I listened to an episode where Raz interviewed the CEO of Lush, Mark Constantine. I love Lush; therefore, I was curious to hear more of the company's back story.

Constantine shared that sometimes the best thing you can do as a company is to think of your future in six-week increments (Raz, 2020).

> **"** Therefore, thinking of a change in six-week increments has supported me as a leader during this time. We may not know what will happen in a year or six months from now, but setting goals in shorter time sections can give us more confidence as a leader. **"**

This way of thinking really struck me, especially as I am leading during COVID-19. Things are changing by the second, and although we are still creating long-term goals as a school community, we must alter our approach. We must be realistic that now, more than ever, things are changing rapidly.

At my school, we have regular collaborative meetings with as many staff members and stakeholders as possible. These meetings help us to gain the further insight needed to continue and shift our goals. For example, we set regular meetings with our:

- Grade Level Teams
- Special Education Team
- Special Area Team
- Special Education Team Leader
- Team Leaders
- Counselors
- Reading Interventionist
- School Support Interventionist
- Building Custodians
- Secretaries
- Nutritional Staff
- Committees
- Our Faculty as a whole
- PTA
- Families to build proactive student support plans

> **INFLUENCE & IMPLEMENT**
>
> - In your daily practice, how do you engage in thinking in short bursts to reach your goals?
> - Once you set short- and long-term goals, how do you make these goals continually visible for your staff?
> - As leaders, we often forget to celebrate small wins. How can we do a better job in this area within our school community? Celebrating others in an authentic and intentional way can help promote continued school growth.

As you can see, we meet with a lot of individuals in a month's time. I am sure you do as well. Each of the meetings is information for me. I use this information to help us stay on our path as a building. During the summer, we as schools create School Improvement Goals which is the anchor of our work. As we meet with stakeholders and staff members, we meet as an administrative team weekly to debrief. Our debriefs are set on the same day, same time, and we do everything in our power to not double book ourselves.

These regular meetings with your team are crucial to process the feelings, information, and data you have handled within the week. Based on our weekly checkpoints, we decide each month if we are getting closer to reaching our School Improvement Plan (SIP), goals or making adjustments to better support students and staff. We have continually made adjustments throughout this school year while still staying true to our goals and big vision.

> ❝we have gained confidence in the work we are doing as a team by sharing the specific celebrations and with our staff. We love making thinking visible for our staff and showing the measures of growth we have made along the way while showcasing our people.❞

In addition,

As leaders, we continually use the data to inform decisions while also consistently accounting for the humans in the equation first.

Thinking in short bursts, whether it is one week, monthly, or six weeks, will help make the long-term action steps more doable. Whatever you decide, ensure you and your team are on the same page and follow through on the said plan. Do what works best for you and your school. Keep your eye on the prize!

▶ WHAT IS WRONG WITH BEING CONFIDENT?

As Demi Lovato sings wonderfully, "What is wrong with being, what's wrong with being, what's wrong with being confident?" I love the song "Confident!" It is a total vibe for me. I jam to that lyric each time I need a boost in myself. Hearing it quickly reminds me that there is indeed nothing wrong with being who you are.

If you are not confident in yourself, no one will be so on your behalf.

As a school leader, confidence is the base point you need to make the hard decisions necessary for your students. These crucial decisions you make now will help paint the future trajectory of your school. Frequently, leaders before us have made poor decisions that can make it hard to turn the tables in a positive direction.

Regardless of your current situation, before you can stay on your path as an individual and school—You need to know what your course even is!

You, as a leader, are called to help your school community do just that.

It is not always easy in a world so politically charged where everyone has an opinion and is not afraid to share it. Of course, we as leaders will always take the feedback of others, but we are still charged with moving our school ahead. Therefore, trust your gut and do only what you can do.

All of your experiences, hardships, and learnings have led you to where you are now.

Do not sell yourself short or feel like the task ahead is too impossible of a feat. Sometimes the obstacles around you can feel impossibly overwhelming. However, even if your school is standing on a rocky foundation, know this:

You have the skills and confidence within you to push through the barriers ahead!

There is nothing wrong with being confident. Own it.

You know what you need to do—Go out and do it!

▶ JUST BE YOU

You are a beautiful blend of culture, memories, traditions, familial life, and previous and current friendships. The beautiful thing about your journey as a leader is that only you can be you. Your identity as a person and as a leader matter; no one can take that away from you.

Each person has a skill set that is to be honored and celebrated.

Celebrate others while still celebrating you and your progress. All the while, do not get distracted! Stay on your path.

Your staff, students, and community will know from the beginning if you are true to yourself long before you do.

Leaders who do their best work do so by staying on their path and becoming an expert on what they do best.

> **"** You will not be a successful leader if you try to emulate another person on their path. Instead, learn from others, grow from others, but stay firm in the foundation of who you are and what you are called to do. **"**

How will you as a leader step into your newfound confidence and forge ahead?

▶ 3 KEY TAKEAWAYS

- Your dream should be yours and no one else's. Follow your path because it speaks to you, not because someone else is living it out.
- There are no quick fixes to stay on the path for you or your school. For any goal you develop, you need to be willing to put in the work required to make it happen.
- Carve time for self-reflection. Self-reflection is the key to getting a solid grip on where you are as a leader. You need this knowledge to decide if your current decisions mesh with who and where you need to be. Begin to love the art form of self-reflection and spread it to all you serve.

References

Mipham, S. (2012). Running with the mind of meditation: Lessons for training body and mind. In *Running with the mind of meditation: Lessons for training body and mind* (pp. 78–79). New York: Three Rivers Press, Harmony.

Poole, C. (2021, April 28). How am I being complicit in educational inequities? / Self-Reflection [Web blog post]. Retrieved May 2, 2021, from https://www.claytonschools.net/Page/21956

Raz, G. (2020, October 4). Lush Cosmetics: Mark Constantine. NPR. How I built this with Guy. Raz. Retrieved from https://podcasts.apple.com/us/podcast/lush-cosmetics-mark-constantine/id1150510297?i=1000493588485

White, M. A. (2020, July 6). Decision fatigue: Effects, causes, signs, and how to combat it. Retrieved May 02, 2021, from https://www.medicalnewstoday.com/articles/decision-fatigue#summary

Live in the Present, Visualize the Future

▶ INTRODUCTION

> **BEFORE YOU START READING**
>
> Within this chapter, you will unpack:
>
> - Findings from the Singapore American School (SAS) as they researched and created a new school mission and vision
> - Your circle of influence and how to make the most out of it
> - Being brave enough to make the difficult decisions that will positively impact students for a lifetime
> - Determining what will set your school apart and why this continual work matters

Life continually shows us how tough it can be to be present at the moment. We are bombarded with facts, statistics, fears, relentless media, and the unknown more than ever before. All of which centers our worries around the future rather than the now.

We constantly wonder: *What will happen next? What is in store for us?*

It can feel like mission impossible to consistently live in the present moment, as both a human being and a school leader. Living in the present is not something that we master once and live happily ever after. Rather, living in the present looks more

DOI: 10.4324/9781003124627-8

> **"With the world ever-changing around us, one thing we can always expect is that there will always be a new now and new normal. As leaders, to properly navigate through this, we will need to model flexibility in our cognitive approach and with our school community."**

like a practice we work to develop every day, in as many moments of our day as possible.

There is an abundant amount to experience in the now. The truth is that the present is the only moment we can count on. We cannot go back in the past, but we can decide to pause and soak in the now.

Education can often feel rigid. Educational systems, procedures, traditions, and the status quo can reign supreme. Some of the rules we live by as educators are often the unwritten ones that we follow, without actively realizing that we are.

Rather than seeing change as an adversary, we can view change as our ally. The global pandemic we have experienced has shown that there will always be a new normal. Therefore, how can we continually embrace the new now while strategically and passionately moving our schools forward?

▶ THE DEDICATION OF SAS

Leaders must have a compelling vision that they can envision while being able to gather those they serve around it. Living in the present yet visualizing an even brighter future is essential for a leader to be confident and successful. Yet, the strategy of visualization is not one we were necessarily trained on as leaders. According to data accumulated by Chief Scientist Evan Sinar, "Over 50 percent of leaders assessed struggle to demonstrate a form of visionary leadership, a larger deficiency percentage than for any other leadership skill. Leaders are consistently unable to vividly paint a compelling picture of the future in a way that inspires others to follow them along a challenging route toward a new reality (Sinar, 2016)."

So, how do we continually adapt our skills in this area?

We first need to see how other successful schools and leaders make their thinking visible. SAS is a phenomenal model for us to reference. SAS has become an international leader for schools in building a strategic focus while creating a solid foundation for the future. The goal of SAS is to cultivate exceptional learners and leaders for the future.

The Superintendent of SAS, Chip Kimball, brought a collaborative team of educators together at his school to research other highly successful and learning progressive schools to develop their strategic vision. Below is a synthesis of their work (Stuart, 2018):

SAS administrators and educators researched and visited over 100 schools in seven countries in one year to challenge their thinking.

1. SAS developed intentional questions to guide their work and research, such as "What do we want to be known for?" and "What will set us apart from other schools?"
2. After their research, SAS decided on three strategic anchors they wanted to embody based on what they witnessed. SAS is committed to ensuring a culture of excellence, extraordinary care, and possibilities.
3. SAS developed a plan to build capacity in executing its three strategic anchors.

When you go to SAS's website (SAS Strategic Focus 2021), you will notice that SAS published their strategic anchors, vision, mission, their five priorities in the current school year, core values, and an interactive video of students to highlight their work. The strategic plan is simple yet thorough, while also being graphically appeasing and student-centered.

The entire team at SAS teamed together in a cooperative and joined to build a school that would be transformational for kids. This did not happen overnight, and it was not done on a whim.

Although we may not have all of the opportunities of SAS, I know I for one cannot afford to visit 100 schools in seven countries. Yet, there are valuable lessons to learn from SAS as a whole.

▶ VISUALIZATION IS KEY

There is often internal pressure that we self-create as leaders to create a powerful mission and vision, but timing is everything.

From my experience, we need to know our school community and do internal research before we can jump in and create.

> **As leaders, we need to pause and reflect on where we are currently, what we are proud of within our school community, while also taking a long hard look at what we need to shift for our kids.**

I used to believe that leaders needed to change their school's mission and vision before they could do the work necessary to shift their school culture, but now I know that is not always the case.

Whether it is your first year in your school or you have been leading at your school community for years, we all need to engage in this practice of reflection. If we do not reflect, we are likely to continue what we are comfortable doing while staying in our self-created echo chamber.

Permit yourself to soak in the knowledge necessary to make the best decisions for your school and students. Have a sense of urgency, but do not rush the important work. All along the way, trust that intuition of yours. Visualize that intuition to make it a reality.

At my school, we are building a voluntary Mission and Vision Team that will engage in our version of the SAS work to build a mission, vision, and value system that we all can get excited about. We have support staff members and certified staff members who are a part of this team as well to move us forward. I believe that having a variety of diverse stakeholders who are committed to the work is crucial to our work at schools.

Yet, before we engaged in this mission and vision work, my goal was to first soak in the strengths of our community and the areas of growth while also accessing how I could confidently support. As a first-year Principal, I invested time in meeting with community members, parents, and staff members within our building to also gain insight on what they were most proud of within our school community and how they wanted to evolve. I also continually engaged with my leadership team, collaborative grade-level teams, reading team, and district experts for insight as well. The wisdom of being surrounded by collaborative teams is one of the best practices you can build as a leader.

Through this, I gathered a meta-analysis of sorts. I congregated anecdotes and experiences from listening to others. In addition, I obtained and analyzed data based on our previous and current school performance and social-emotional data. Gathering this information and hearing others out helped me to visualize how we can build upon our future as a community.

I truly believe that visualizing our futures is the first step to making our goals a reality; if we cannot see them, how can we embody them?

What do you currently visualize for the future of your school? How can you rally those around you to engage in this work as well?

▶ YOUR CIRCLE OF INFLUENCE

What is your circle of influence and who is in it?

Your circle of influence refers to the area of your work or life where you can make changes. Not the area that you wish you could make changes, but the area where you actually can.

It is easy to get lost while determining what is in your circle of influence and what is not. Setting boundaries on your influence can be one of the most difficult tasks. We often want to bite off more than we can chew. Yet, if we are not aware of our boundaries, we can become resentful of the items that we cannot change.

We can either blame our lack of growth on outside influences or choose to find what is in our circle of influence. Let's choose to emphasize what we do have control over.

To illustrate, you may not be able to travel to visit schools around the world to expand your thinking, but you definitely can use your influence in other ways. Do not get me wrong; I love visiting schools across my state to see the innovative initiatives they are taking on. But throughout our hopes in gaining new viewpoints, do not also forget to see the gifts that are in your school community.

> "Whether you realize it or not, you do have a circle of influence and that influence is around you all the time. How can you directly cultivate your circle of influence to help your school progress?"

CONFIDENT SCHOOL LEADERS

Ideas to Ponder:

- As you continually push your school forward, determine what is urgent and not urgent. You may have the passion and work ethic to influence many areas now, but not everything is urgent. Decipher what is crucial to your school mission now.

- How can you help build confidence in others and promote their God-given strengths? Students and staff members alike need to feel valued by their leaders and schools.
- Be clear in what you expect from those you serve. People cannot read your mind and would rather know what is on your heart and mind.
- Just as you and your staff members should know your school's vision, mission, and values, they should also know your value system as a leader. Do you actively promote what you stand for? Do you know what your staff members and students stand for as well?
- Does your circle of influence only include those who look like you? Reflect upon your unconscious biases to determine how you lift up diverse voices. As Yrthya Dinzey-Flores, a Global Leader in Social Impact Strategies, states, "The value of a diverse team is its capacity to challenge the norm or group think and thus boost organizational performance and improve decision-making."

As you reflect and ponder the ideas and questions above, never forget that your circle of influence is all around you, but that also starts and ends with yourself.

You are the greatest circle of influence you will ever have.

▶ HAVE THE CONFIDENCE TO DO WHAT IS NECESSARY

> "Old ways will not open new doors."

We often know what we need to do to transform our school, but can lack the support or confidence to run with it. When change is inadvertently viewed as bad, even if it is what is best for students, it can oppress those who are dedicated to making change a reality.

As I looked through potential images and photographs for the cover of this book, *The Confident School Leader*, I was bombarded by images of superheroes, men climbing cliffs and walking tightropes, and images of people flexing their muscles. Confidence is always made to seem superhuman or unattainable. Yet, what I am constantly reminded of is that you do not need a cape to have confidence. Instead, confidence is simply being who you are. Step into it and own it!

We are often looking for outside sources and consultants to help solve the array of complex problems that we face in schools. Yet, as Paul Senge shares in his book with collaborators, *Schools that Learn*, "In the long run, the insiders are the only people who can make and sustain the fundamental changes necessary to solve the problem (Cambron-McCabe, Lucas, Smith, Dutton, & Kleiner, 2012)."

> **"**We must build collective efficacy and shift the burden of solving the problem to those within the school organization.**"**

Senge also shares a metaphor in reading specialists at schools to further prove this idea (Cambron-McCabe, Lucas, Smith, Dutton, & Kleiner, 2012). If reading specialists, for example, do not help to promote reading skills and proficiencies in the teachers within their schools, they are not helping to build capable teachers. Instead, the reading specialists will always be the sole experts and the responsibility of building strong student readers will always rely on the specialists.

As we continually move forward in gaining confidence in ourselves as leaders, we must also promote confidence within our schools by helping our teachers and staff to build upon their skills and repertoire. I believe it is the leader's responsibility to provide high support paired with high expectations to be the best we can be for our kids. It is then the responsibility of other staff members in the building to do their part as well. If one is committed to the school's continued growth, it will always show through their actions and practices.

Being committed to constructive and lasting change as a leader means responding to potential resistance like a tree. In trees, the wind makes them stronger and helps them to continually stay planted in the ground while being connected to other trees in their network. Resistance has the same benefits to us as a leader. It makes us stronger while helping us stay connected to the same mission and vision as us.

> **"**Have the confidence to not blend in and to sway to the conformities of the world around you. Be brave enough to make the hard decisions; only you know what those decisions are. These choices that you make now can elevate students to be limitless.**"**

Your students and our students deserve nothing less. You as the leader are the gatekeeper to do what is right for kids. What you permit and what you do not will set the stage for our kids in the present moment, and in the years to come.

Visualize the future that our students deserve and be confident enough to create that destiny. Your influence matters.

▶ SELF-LOVE IS YOUR STRENGTH

As we live in the present and visualize the future for our schools we must do the same in our personal lives as well. I am incredibly passionate about caring for ourselves, just as we care for our students. Leaders who embody self-love are often those who love the people they serve the most.

Self-love is an area that I am continually working on as a person. But, I have found great peace recently by spending time in the outdoors, therapy, deleting my social media apps for a set period of time, practicing restorative yoga, and writing and journaling. Taking this time for myself, which is more of a rare occurrence than I dare to admit, helps to make me feel centered and grounded.

When I spend time in the present moment for me I feel repurposed, like someone pushed a reset button on my soul.

What I continually remind myself is that tomorrow will take care of itself and bring enough worries for that day. Therefore, as leaders, let's continue to promote self-love today for ourselves, students, and others.

Today and every day, my challenge for you is to be present and to cherish this moment. In this present moment, show gratitude for what you do have rather than what you are lacking. In many ways, it is easy for us to see what is missing from our lives. Yet, living from a place of absence will never bring you quietude. Instead, see the abundance that you have today.

Remember: You are strong. You have roots of confidence that are firmly wrapped around you. You have what it takes to

---

INFLUENCE & IMPLEMENT

- Your influence is wrapped up in those you love, yet it also blooms within. Keep in mind: Your influence will grow within you and expand to others.
- You cannot care for the present moment if you do not bring attention to yourself.
- In the same breath, you are more likely to visualize the future if you are at peace in the now. *How can you find the stillness and purpose in this moment?*

navigate the future ahead. In the meantime, find your slice of joy in the moment and love who you are.

When you love yourself, it shows. Our students will thrive seeing leaders who love themselves, quirks, oddities, and all. How can you influence others if you do not love yourself and the influence you have to offer? Self-love is your strength.

▶ WHAT WILL SET YOUR SCHOOL APART?

You are a walking, breathing part of your school's mission. Do you feel this in your soul? Do you own it?

> **“** The ripple effects from your schools' efforts today will have no bounds. **”**

All of our efforts as leaders will have ripple effects on the world around us (Eller & Carlson, 2009). Our influence comes with a great responsibility to care for others. We were created to make a difference and within us we have the power to change the world. I truly believe that educators are the adaptable learning experts that maximize and accelerate human potential (Frey, Hattie, & Fisher, 2018). Human potential is our only limitless resource.

Above all the initiatives and what is expected of us, I want my school, and yours, to be known for being safe places that elevate students for who they are while guiding them to be who they hope to be. I want our school communities to truly believe in our heart of hearts that it is possible to create such spaces.

> **“** Our goal is to not be the best; it is about being better than who we were yesterday. **”**

In every regard, leadership demands both relentless optimism and confidence.

Education is the greatest line of work in the world, and the future of our students, and their present, is in our hands. Let us always remain inspired.

You and I as leaders have the promise to create schools that are forward-thinking, transformational to learning, and centered in love.

When you close this book and continue your journey of leadership, how will you walk

> **“** Pessimism and hopelessness for public education will not ever win in my book nor have a place in our schools. Let us rally together, with confidence to make a lasting impact on schools that will bring ripples for a lifetime. **”**

in confidence to both you and your school's purpose? Step into your unwavering confidence and make your mark.

If not us, who?

▶ 3 KEY TAKEAWAYS

- The SAS took pride in their mission and vision work to help propel their school forward. They asked themselves, "What do we want to be known for," created strategic anchors they wanted to embody as a community, and developed a plan to build capacity in this work to make their dreams a reality. It is an inspiration for many to see SAS's drive for continued growth and student success.
- Your circle of influence is powerful. The difference you can make will be spread to those within your circle. Invest the time to building confidence in others and their skills. Now, watch as your circle continually expands positively over time!
- Be committed to lasting change and progress. Have the confidence to move your school in a brand-new direction for kids. This commitment will mean facing potential resistance like a tree. Let the wind makes you stronger, stay planted in the ground, all while staying rooted with the educators in your network. Do the work that matters.

References

Cambron-McCabe, N., Lucas, T., Smith, B., Dutton, J., & Kleiner, A. (2012). Schools that learn: a FIFTH discipline fieldbook for educators, parents, and everyone who cares about education. In P. M. Senge (Author), *Schools that learn: A fifth discipline fieldbook for educators, parents, and everyone who cares about education* (pp. 377–378). London: Nicholas Brealey.

Eller, J., & Carlson, H. C. (2009). So now you're the superintendent! In *So, Now You're the Superintendent!* (pp. 174–175). Thousand Oaks, CA: Corwin Press.

Frey, N., Hattie, J., & Fisher, D. (2018). *Developing assessment-capable visible learners: Grades K-12: Maximizing skill, will, and thrill.* Thousand Oaks, CA: Corwin, A SAGE Company.

SAS Strategic Focus. (2021). Retrieved May 13, 2021, from https://www.sas.edu.sg/about-us/strategic-focus

Sinar, E. (2016, May 29). To become a more visionary leader, become stronger at visualization [Web blog post]. Retrieved May 6, 2021, from https://medium.com/@EvanSinar/to-become-a-more-visionary-leader-become-stronger-at-visualization-4c629e133eb1

Stuart, T. S. (2018). Personalized learning in a PLC at WORK: Student agency through the four critical questions. In *Personalized learning in a PLC at Work: Student agency through the four critical questions* (pp. 171–174). Bloomington, IN: Solution Tree Press.

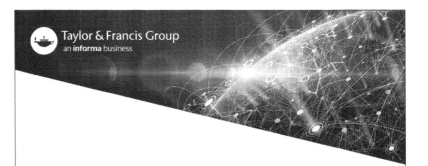

Printed in the United States
by Baker & Taylor Publisher Services